David Grann

The Old Man and the Gun

David Grann is a staff writer at *The New Yorker* and the bestselling author of *The Lost City of Z* and *Killers of the Flower Moon*, a National Book Award finalist. Both were chosen as best books of the year by *The New York Times*, *The Washington Post*, and other publications. Grann is also the author of the essay collection *The Devil and Sherlock Holmes*. His work has garnered several honors for outstanding journalism, including a George Polk Award and an Edgar Award.

www.davidgrann.com

The Old Man and the Gun

The

Old Man

and the

Gun

And Other Tales of True Crime

David Grann

**SIMON &
SCHUSTER**

London · New York · Sydney · Toronto · New Delhi

A CBS COMPANY

These essays are taken from *The Devil and Sherlock Holmes*
First published in the United States by Doubleday,
a division of Penguin Random House LLC, 2010
First published in Great Britain by Simon & Schuster UK Ltd, 2010
This edition published in Great Britain by Simon & Schuster UK Ltd, 2018
A CBS COMPANY

Copyright © David Grann, 2010

The right of David Grann to be identified as the author of
this work has been asserted in accordance with the
Copyright, Designs and Patents Act, 1988.

The pieces in this work first published, in slightly different form,
in *The New Yorker*: 'The Old Man and the Gun' on 27 January 2003 'True Crime'
on 11 and 18 February 2008; and 'The Chameleon' on 11 August 2008.

1 3 5 7 9 10 8 6 4 2

Simon & Schuster UK Ltd
1st Floor
222 Gray's Inn Road
London WC1X 8HB

www.simonandschuster.co.uk
www.simonandschuster.com.au
www.simonandschuster.co.in

Simon & Schuster Australia, Sydney
Simon & Schuster India, New Delhi

The author and publishers have made all reasonable
efforts to contact copyright-holders for permission, and apologise
for any omissions or errors in the form of credits given.
Corrections may be made to future printings.

A CIP catalogue record for this book is available from the British Library

Paperback ISBN: 978-1-4711-8166-5
eBook ISBN: 978-1-4711-8167-2

Pr

that is ⌐   rest
Stewards   ⌐tion.
Our ⌐   ⌐.

Contents

The Old Man and the Gun

The Old Man and the Gun

Just before Forrest Tucker turned seventy-nine, he went to work for the last time. Although he was still a striking-looking man, with intense blue eyes and swept-back white hair, he had a growing list of ailments, including high blood pressure and burning ulcers. He had already had a quadruple bypass, and his wife encouraged him to settle into their home in Pompano Beach, Florida, a peach-colored house on the edge of a golf course which they'd purchased for their retirement. There was a place nearby where they could eat prime rib and dance on Saturday nights with other seniors for $15.50 a person, and even a lake where Tucker could sit by the shore and practice his saxophone.

But on this spring day in 1999, while his neighbors were on the fairway or tending to their grandchildren, he drove to the Republic Security Bank in Jupiter, about fifty miles from his home. Tucker, who took pride in his appearance, was dressed all in white: white pants with a sharp crease, a white sports shirt, white suède shoes, and a shimmering white ascot.

He paused briefly in front of the A.T.M. and pulled the ascot up around his face, bandit style. He then reached into a canvas bag, took out an old U.S. Army Colt .45, and burst into the bank. He went up to the first teller and said, "Put your money on the counter. All of it."

He flashed the gun so that everyone could see it. The teller laid several packets of fives and twenties on the counter, and Tucker inspected them for exploding dye packs. Checking his watch, he turned to the next teller and said, "Get over here. You, too."

Then he gathered up the thick packets—more than five thousand dollars—and hurried to the door. On his way out, he looked back at the two tellers. "Thank you," he said. "Thank you."

He drove to a nearby lot, where he had left a "safe" car, a red Grand Am that couldn't be traced to him. After wiping down the stolen "hot" car with a rag, he threw his belongings inside the Grand Am. They included a .357 Magnum, a sawed-off .30 carbine, two black nylon caps, a holster, a can of Mace, a pair of Smith & Wesson handcuffs, two rolls of black electrical tape, a police badge, five AAA batteries, a police scanner, a glass cutter, gloves, and a fishing cap. There was also a small bottle of medicine for his heart. No one seemed to notice him, and he went home, making what appeared to be a clean getaway.

After a brief stop to count the money, he got back in the car and headed out again. As he approached the golf course, the bills neatly stacked beside him, he noticed an unmarked car on his tail. He turned onto another street, just to make sure. There it was again. Then he spotted a police car pulling out behind him. He hit the gas as hard as he could, trying to outmaneuver them, turning left, then right, right, then left. He went past the North Pompano Baptist Church and the Kraeer Funeral Home, past a row of pink one-story houses with speedboats in the driveways, until he found himself on a dead-end street. As he spun around, he saw that a police car was barricading the road. One of the officers, Captain James Chinn, was reaching for his shotgun. There was a small gap between Chinn's car and a wooden fence, and Tucker, his body pitched forward in his seat, sped toward it. Chinn, who had spent almost two decades as a detective, later said he had never seen anything like it: the white-haired figure barrelling toward him seemed to be smiling, as if he were enjoying the showdown. Then, as the car skidded over the embankment, Tucker lost control and hit a palm tree. The air bags inflated, pinning him against the seat.

The police were stunned when they realized that the man they had apprehended was not only seventy-eight years old—he looked, according to Chinn, "as if he had just come from an Early Bird Special"—but one of the most notorious stickup men of the twentieth century. Over a career that spanned more than six decades, he had also become perhaps the greatest escape artist of his generation, a human contortionist who had broken out of nearly every prison he was confined in.

One day in 2002, I went to meet Tucker in Fort Worth, Texas, where he was being held in a prison medical center after pleading guilty to one count of robbery and receiving a thirteen-year sentence. The hospital, an old yellow brick building with a red tiled roof, was on top of a hill and set back off the main road, surrounded by armed guards and razor wire. I was handed a notice that said no "weapons," "ammunition," or "metal cutting tools" were allowed, and then escorted through a series of chambers—each door sealing behind us before the next one opened—until I arrived in an empty waiting room.

Before long, a man appeared in a wheelchair pushed by a guard. He wore brown prison fatigues and a green jacket with a turned-up collar. His figure was twisted forward, as if he had tried to contort it one last time and it had frozen in place. As he rose from the wheelchair, he said, "It's a pleasure to meet you. Forrest Tucker."

His voice was gentle, with a soft Southern lilt. After

he extended his hand, he made his way slowly over to a wooden table with the help of a walker. "I'm sorry we have to meet here," he said, waiting for me to sit first.

Captain Chinn had told me that he had never met such a gracious criminal: "If you see him, tell him Captain Chinn says hi." Even a juror who helped convict him once remarked, "You got to hand it to the guy—he's got style."

"So what do you want to know?" Tucker said. "I've been in prison all my life, except for the times I've broken out. I was born in 1920, and I was in jail by the time I was fifteen. I'm eighty-one now and I'm still in jail, but I've broken out eighteen times successfully and twelve times unsuccessfully. There were plenty of other times I planned to escape, but there's no point in me telling you about them."

As we sat in a corner by a window overlooking the prison yard, it was hard to imagine that this man's career had featured wanted posters and midnight escapes. His fingers were knotted like bamboo, and he wore bifocals.

"What I mean by a successful escape is to elude custody," he continued, squinting out the window. "Maybe they'd eventually get me, but I got away at least for a few minutes."

He pointed to the places along his arm where he had been shot while trying to flee. "I still have part of a bullet in me," he said. "They all opened up on me and hit me three times—in both shoulders with M16 rifles, and with buckshot in the legs."

His voice sounded dry, and I offered to buy him a drink from the vending machine. He followed me and peered through the glass, without touching it. He chose a Dr Pepper. "That's kind of like cherry soda, isn't it?"

He seemed pleased. When I gave him the drink, he glanced at the candy bars, and I asked him if he wanted anything else. "If it's not too much trouble," he said, "I'd like a Mounds."

After he finished eating, he began to tell me what he called "the true story of Forrest Tucker." He spoke for hours, and when he grew tired he offered to continue the next morning. During our conversations, which went on for several days, we always sat in the corner by the window, and after a while he would cough slightly and I would offer to buy him a drink. Each time, he followed me to the machine, as the guard watched from a distance. It was only during the last trip to the machine, when I dropped some money, that I noticed his eyes were moving over everything—the walls, the windows, the guard, the fences, the razor wire. It occurred to me that Tucker, escape artist par excellence, had been using our meetings to case the joint.

"The first time I broke out of the can I was only fifteen," Tucker told me. "At fifteen, you're pretty fast."

It was the spring of 1936, and he had been incarcerated for stealing a car in Stuart, Florida, a small town along the St. Lucie River which had been devastated during the Depression. He told the police that he took it "just for a thrill," but as he sat in jail the thrill gave way to panic, and when a jailer removed his chains he darted out. Several days later, a deputy discovered him in an orange grove, eating a piece of fruit. "That was escape No. 1," Tucker says. "Such as it was."

The sheriff decided to transfer him to reform school. During his brief flight, however, Tucker had slipped a half-dozen hacksaw blades through the cell window to a group of boys he had met inside. "They hadn't broken out yet and still had the blades," he says. That night, after sawing a bar, he slithered out, helping two other boys squeeze through the tiny opening.

Unlike the others, Tucker knew the area. As a kid, he had spent a fair amount of time by the river, and it was in the river that the police found him and another boy, about an hour later, hiding with just their noses above water. The next day, the Stuart *Daily News* detailed his exploits under the headline "TRIO ESCAPE BY SAW-ING BARS OF CELL LAST NIGHT . . . SUPPLIED WITH HACK-SAWS, COLD CHISELS AND FILES BY BOY."

"That was escape No. 2," Tucker says. "A brief one."

Like the outlaws he read about in dime novels who were forced into banditry by some perceived injustice, Tucker says that "the legend of Forrest Tucker" began on the morning when he was unfairly sent away for only a minor theft. The story, which he repeated even as a boy, eventually spread throughout the town, and over time the details became more ornate, the theft more minor. Morris Walton, who used to play with Tucker as a child, says, "My sense is he spent his life in jail for stealing a bicycle and simply trying to escape. If he became bad, it was only because the system made him that way."

What Walton knew of Tucker's upbringing reinforced that impression. His father was a heavy-equipment operator who disappeared when Tucker was six. While his mother struggled in menial jobs in Miami, Tucker was sent to live with his grandmother, who was the tender of the bridge in Stuart. There he built canoes and sailboats out of scrap metal and wood, which he gathered along the riverbank, and taught himself to play the saxophone and the clarinet. "It wasn't like I needed a father to order me around," he says.

But as his reputation for cleverness grew, so did his rap sheet. By his sixteenth birthday, it included charges of "breaking and entering" and "simple larceny." After he escaped from reform school and fled to Georgia, he was sentenced to "be placed and confined at labor in the chain gang." Like all new inmates, he was taken to the blacksmith, where a chain was riveted around both of his ankles. The steel gradually ate into the skin, a condition known as shackle poisoning.

"The guards would give you the first three days to let you get your hands broken in with calluses," Tucker recalls. "But after that the walking boss would punish you, hit you with his cane or fist. And if you didn't work hard enough the guards would take you in the bathroom and tie your hands behind your back and put a pressure hose in your face and hold it there until you'd sputter and you couldn't breathe."

Although Tucker was released after only six months, he was soon convicted again, for stealing another car, and sentenced to ten years. By now, "we see a man who has been thoroughly cast out by society," Tucker's lawyer later wrote in a court motion. "Marked as a criminal at seventeen years old and constantly railroaded through judicial proceedings without the benefit of counsel, Forrest Tucker was becoming an angry young man." Tucker himself says, "The die was cast." In photographs taken after he was paroled at the age of twenty-four, his hair is cut short and he has on a white T-shirt; his once slender arms are coiled with muscles. His eyes are piercing. People who knew him say that he was extraordinarily charismatic—that girls flocked around him—but they also noted a growing reservoir of anger. "I think he had this desperate need to show the world that he was *somebody*," one of his relatives says.

At first, Tucker sought work playing the saxophone in big bands around Miami, and he seemed to have harbored ambitions of becoming another Glenn Miller. Nothing came of it, though, and, after a brief failed marriage, he put away his sax and got himself a gun.

The outlaw, in the American imagination, is a subject of romance—a "good" bad man, he is typically a master of escape, a crack shot, a ladies' man. In 1915, when the police asked the train robber Frank Ryan why he did it, he replied, "Bad companions and dime novels. Jesse James was my favorite hero."

When Tucker was growing up, during the Great Depression, the appeal of bank robbers, fuelled by widespread anger over defaults and foreclosures, was reaching its zenith. After the F.B.I. gunned down John Dillinger, in 1934, droves descended on the scene, mopping up his blood with their clothes. At least ten Hollywood films were devoted to Dillinger's life; one of them exclaimed, "His Story Is Written in Bullets, Blood and Blondes!"

Because the holdup demands a public performance, it tends to draw a certain personality: bold, vainglorious, reckless. At the same time, most bank robbers know that the society that revels in their exploits will ultimately demand their elimination, by incarceration or death. "They'll get me," Pretty Boy Floyd once said. "Sooner or later, I'll go down full of lead. That's how it will end."

Indeed, by the time Tucker set out to become an

outlaw, in the late nineteen-forties, most of the legendary stickup men had already been gunned down. Still,
he began to imitate their style, dressing in chalk-striped
suits and two-tone shoes, and he would stand in front of
a mirror, pointing a gun at his own reflection. Finally,
on September 22, 1950, with a handkerchief tied over
his face and a gun drawn in the style of Jesse James, he
strode into a bank in Miami and made off with $1,278.
A few days later, he went back to the same place, this
time for the entire safe. He was apprehended as he was
trying to crack it open with a blowtorch on the roadside.

His career seemed even more fleeting than that of
most bank robbers, but in the county jail Tucker decided
he was more than an ordinary stickup man. "It didn't
matter to me if they gave me five years, ten years, or life,"
he says. "I was an escape artist."

He searched the prison for what he called "the weak
spot." One day around Christmas, after weeks of looking, he began to moan in pain. The authorities rushed
him to the hospital, where doctors removed his appen-
dix. ("A small price to pay," Tucker says.) While conva-
lescing, still chained to his bed, he started to work on the
shackles. He had taught himself how to pick a lock using
almost anything—a pen, a paper clip, a piece of wire,
nail clippers, a watch spring—and after a few minutes he
walked out, unnoticed.

He made his way to California, where he went on a

spree of robberies, hurtling over counters, pointing his gun, and declaring, "I mean business!" He wore bright checkered suits and sped away in a flamboyant getaway car with tubes along the sides. He even talked like a character in pulp fiction. "This is a stickup, girls," he once said, according to witnesses. "I've got a gun. Be quiet and you won't get hurt."

Hoping to improve his take, Tucker began to cast about for a partner. "I didn't want any nuts or rats," he says, adding, "I'm from the old school." In the end, he found an ex-con named Richard Bellew, a tall, handsome thief with a high I.Q. and wavy black hair. Like Tucker, Bellew modelled himself on the stickup men of the nineteen-thirties, and he ran with a stage dancer named Jet Blanca. But Tucker chose him for another reason: "He always let me count the dough."

They began to hit one bank after another. After one heist, witnesses said the last thing they saw was a row of suits hanging in the back seat of the getaway car. The heists, which continued for two years, dominated the local headlines, often preempting coverage of the 1952 Presidential election and the McCarthy hearings. Tucker and Bellew were depicted as "armed men" who "terrorized" their "victims," but also as "dramatically attired" "hold-up artists" who "expertly stripped" the tellers of cash, leaving behind "only an impression of competent banditry . . . and one getaway car."

On March 20, 1953, more than two years after Tucker's escape from the hospital, F.B.I. agents surrounded him as he was retrieving loot from a safe-deposit box in San Francisco. Then they went to search the place Tucker had listed as his residence. There, in a spacious apartment in San Mateo, they found a young blond woman who said she had never heard of Forrest Tucker. She was married to a wealthy songwriter, she said, who commuted daily to the city, and they had just moved into a bigger apartment to make room for their five-month-old son. Her husband's name, she told the police, was Richard Bellew. Yet when the officers showed Shirley Bellew a photograph of the bank robber and longtime prison fugitive Forrest Tucker, she burst into tears. "I can't believe it," she said. "He was such a good man, such a good provider."

She recalled how her husband would come home every night and play with their baby, whom they had named Rick Bellew, Jr. "What's going to become of our little baby?" she asked. "What's his name going to be?"

"Let me tell you about Alcatraz," Tucker said one day as he sat in the corner of the visiting room, his walker resting against his leg. He had spread a napkin out in front of him and was eating a meatball hero I'd brought him and sipping a Dr Pepper. "There were only fifteen hundred and seventy-six people who ever went there. I was No. 1047."

Alcatraz, or "the Rock," had been converted from a military prison in 1934 as a way to confine the country's most notorious criminals, including George (Machine Gun) Kelly, Robert Stroud (the Birdman of Alcatraz), and Mickey Cohen. At least half of the inmates had previously attempted to break out of other prisons. Surrounded by the freezing San Francisco Bay and its deadly currents, it was built to be escape-proof. Al Capone, who was sent there in 1934, is said to have told the warden, "It looks like Alcatraz has got me licked."

Tucker arrived on September 3, 1953. He was thirty-three. He had been sentenced to thirty years. In his prison photo, he still has on a jacket and tie; his brown hair is brushed back with a touch of oil; he is slightly unshaved but still striking. Within moments, he was stripped naked, and a medical attendant probed his ears and nose and mouth and rectum, searching for any tools or weapons. He was given a blue chambray shirt with his number stamped on it and a pair of trousers, as well as a cap, a peacoat, a bathrobe, three pairs of socks, two handkerchiefs, a pair of shoes, and a raincoat. His cell was so narrow that he could reach out and touch both sides at the same time. "It was so cold in the cellblock you had to sleep with your coat and hat to stay warm," Tucker says.

As he lay in bed, he says, he thought about his wife and child. He remembered the first time he met Shirley Storz, at an event for singles in Oakland. He remembered how they skied at Lake Tahoe and were married in a small ceremony in September of 1951, how she sang in a choral group, and how he'd sit and listen for hours. And he remembered his son being born. "We loved each other," Tucker says of his wife. "I didn't know how to explain to her the truth—that this was my way of life."

Several weeks after he arrived, a guard roused him from his cell and led him into a tiny room that had a small window. Peering through it, he saw his wife sitting on the other side. He picked up the phone. "It was hard to talk," he recalls. "We had to look at each other through a piece of glass. She told me she had to make a life for herself. I said, 'The best thing you can do is make a life for you and our son.' I told her, 'I won't bother you no matter what, no matter how much I want to. I won't ring your phone.'" A few months later, he received notice that their marriage had been annulled.

By now, Tucker had developed several maxims, including "The more security, the more bizarre the method of escape must be." He began to concoct elaborate schemes with a fellow inmate named Teddy Green, an escape artist and bank robber who had once dressed as a priest to elude the police and had broken out of the state penitentiary by shipping himself out in a box of rags.

Along with another inmate, they started smuggling tools from their prison jobs, hiding them in the laundry, and planting pieces of steel wool on other prisoners to set off the metal detectors, so that the guards assumed they were broken. They carved holes in their toilet bowls and tucked the tools inside, putting putty over them. At night, they used the tools to tunnel through the floor, planning to go out by means of the basement.

One day, according to internal prison records, a prisoner in solitary suggested that guards examine the cell toilets; soon a full-scale search was launched. A warden's report summed up the findings:

> The result of the shakedown of these toilets was the blow torch as I have mentioned, a bar spreader, a pair of side cutters, a brace and some bits . . . a screwdriver and one or two pieces of wire and a piece of carborundum stone.

All three prisoners were labelled "very dangerous escape risks" and locked in the Treatment Unit, better known as "the hole."

"I remember walking in with no clothes or shoes on," Tucker says. "The steel floor was so cold it hurt to touch it. The only way to stay warm was to keep walking." One night, he heard a haunting sound through the window. He couldn't see anyone outside, but he heard voices from below. They were the guards' children, singing carols. "It was the first children's voices I had heard in years," he says. "It was Christmas Eve."

As the time passed, Tucker began to teach himself the law, and before long he was deluging the court with appeals, which he wrote in a slanting methodical print. Although a prosecutor later dismissed one of his writs as pure "fantasy," he was granted a hearing in November of 1956. According to Tucker, as well as court records, the night before his court appearance, while being held in the county jail, he complained of pains in his kidneys and was rushed to the hospital. Guards were stationed at every door. When no one was looking, Tucker broke a pencil and stabbed his ankle. Because of the wound, the guards removed his leg irons, strapping him to the gurney with his hands cuffed. As he was being wheeled into the X-ray room, Tucker leaped up, overpowered two guards, and ran out the door. For several hours, he enjoyed the fresh air and the sight of ordinary people. He was apprehended, still in his hospital gown and hand-cuffs, in the middle of a cornfield.

The brief escape, for which he was tried and convicted, enhanced his reputation as an escape artist. Yet it was not for another twenty-three years, after Tucker had been released and arrested again for armed robbery, that he made his greatest escape. In the summer of 1979, while at San Quentin, a maximum-security facility that jutted out into the ocean and was known among cons as "the gladiator school," Tucker took a job in the prison industries and, with the help of two other inmates, John Waller and William McGirk, secretly gathered together scraps of wood and sheets of Formica, which they cut into strange shapes and hid under tarps. From the electrical shop, they spirited away two six-foot poles and several buckets. Then, in the furniture workshop, they found the final pieces: plastic dustcovers, paint, and tape, which they stored in boxes labelled "Office Supplies."

On August 9th, after months of preparation, Tucker exchanged nods with both of his confederates in the yard, signalling that everything was ready. While Waller and McGirk stood watch outside the lumber shop, Tucker drew on his childhood experience and began to fashion the pieces into a fourteen-foot kayak. "A hammer was too loud, so I had to use only tape and bolts," Tucker says. He had just enough paint for one side of the craft, the side that would face the guard towers, and as the others urged him to hurry he stencilled on it "Rub-a-Dub-Dub." Waller, who called the fifty-nine-year-old Tucker "the old man," later told a reporter from the Los Angeles *Times,* "The boat was beautiful; I wish my eyes were as blue as that boat."

They wore sailor hats and sweatshirts that Tucker had painted bright orange, with the logo of the Marin

Yacht Club, which he had seen on the boats that sailed by. When the guard wasn't looking, they hurriedly put the kayak into the water. As they set out, the winds were blowing more than twenty miles an hour, and massive swells began to swamp the kayak. "The boat didn't leak a drop," Waller said. "We could have paddled to Australia. It was those damn waves over the side. When we finally reached the edge of the property at Q"—San Quentin— "the son of a bitch sank."

A guard in one of the towers spotted them clinging to the upside-down craft, kicking to shore, and asked if they needed help. They said they were fine, and, as if to prove it, McGirk held up his wrist and yelled, "We just lost a couple of oars, but my Timex is still running!" The guard, unaware that three prisoners were missing, laughed and went back to his lookout.

California soon unleashed a statewide manhunt. Meanwhile, police in Texas and Oklahoma began to report a strange series of holdups. They all had the same M.O.: three or four men would stroll into a grocery store or a bank, flash a gun, demand the money, and speed away in a stolen car. Witnesses invariably noted that they were all, by the standards of the trade, old men. One even wore what appeared to be a hearing aid. The authorities compared them to the elderly thieves in the film "Going in Style," and dubbed them "the Over-the-Hill Gang."

"That was when I was really a good robber," Tucker tells me. He is careful not to admit to any particular crime ("I don't know if they still have jurisdiction") or implicate any of his living partners ("Some of them are still out there"), but he says that by the age of sixty he had at last mastered the art of the holdup.

One day, while we were sitting in the prison visiting room, Tucker leaned forward in his chair and began to teach me how to rob a bank. "First of all, you want a place near the highway," he said, putting on his bifocals, his eyes blinking as if he were imagining a particular layout. "Then you need to case it—you can't just storm in. You need to size it up, know it like your own home."

"In the old days, the stickup men were like cowboys," he continued. "They would just go in shooting, yelling for everyone to lie down. But to me violence is the first sign of an amateur." The best holdup men, in his view, were like stage actors, able to hold a room by the sheer force of their personality. Some even wore makeup and practiced getting into character. "There is an art to robbing a bank if you do it right," Tucker said. Whereas he once cultivated a flamboyant image, he later developed, he said, a subtler, more "natural" style.

"O.K., the tools," he pressed on. Ideally, he said, you needed nail polish or superglue to cover your fingertips ("You can wear gloves, but in warmer climates they only draw attention"), a glass cutter, a holster, a canvas bag ("big enough for the dough"), and a gun ("a .38 or semi-

automatic, or whatever you can get your hands on").
He said the gun was just "a prop," but essential to any
operation.

There was one other thing, he said after a pause. It
was the key to the success of the Over-the-Hill Gang
and what he still called "the Forrest Tucker trademark":
the hearing aid. It was actually a police scanner, he said,
which he wired through his shirt; that way, he would
know if any silent alarms had been triggered.

He removed a napkin from his pocket and wiped the
sweat from his forehead. "Once you've got your cool car
parked nearby, you've got your radio, your hands are covered with gloves or superglue, you walk in. Go right up
to the manager. Say, 'Sit down.' Never pull the gun—just
flash it. Tell him calmly you're here to rob the bank and
it better go off without a hitch. Don't run from the bank
unless you're being shot at, 'cause it only shows something is going on. Just walk to the hot car, real calm, then
drive to the cool car. Rev it up, and you're gone."

After he finished, he seemed satisfied. "I've just given
you a manual on how to rob a bank," he said. He reflected
on this for a moment, then added, "No one can teach you
the craft. You can only learn by doing."

A forty-year-old sergeant on the Austin police force,
John Hunt, was assigned to investigate the mysterious
holdups of the Over-the-Hill Gang. "They were the

most professional, successful robbers that I ever encountered in all my years on the force," Hunt, who is now retired after a thirty-year career, told me. "They had more experience in robbery than we had catching them."

Then a chain-smoker with a drooping mustache and a slight paunch, Hunt spent long days trying to catch the gang. With the advent of high-tech security, there were fewer and fewer traditional bank robbers; most were desperate drug addicts who made off with only a few thousand dollars before they were caught. The members of the Over-the-Hill Gang seemed to defy not just their age but their era. "They'd get up every day and be on the job," Hunt said. "Just as a welder gets good at welding, or a writer gets good over the years by writing, these guys learned from their mistakes."

In a one-year span, the Over-the-Hill Gang was suspected in at least sixty robberies in Oklahoma and Texas—twenty in the Dallas–Fort Worth area alone. The gang was also believed to be responsible for holdups in New Mexico, Arizona, and Louisiana. "SENIOR CITIZENS STRIKE AGAIN," one headline blared. "MIDDLE-AGED BANDITS PUZZLE DETECTIVES," another read.

In December of 1980, Hunt and forty other law-enforcement officers from at least three states held a conference in Dallas to figure out how to stop them. "You can't say how many lives they altered by sticking a gun in someone's face," a former F.B.I. agent told me.

Tucker seemed unable to stop, no matter how much money he accumulated. Although there are no official estimates, Tucker—relying on an array of aliases, including Robert Tuck MacDougall, Bob Stone, Russell Johns, Ralph Pruitt, Forrest Brown, J. C. Tucker, and Ricky Tucker—is believed over his career to have stolen millions of dollars, a fleet of sports cars, a bag of yen, and one Sambo's wooden nickel. In the spring of 1983, he embarked on his most audacious heist yet: robbing a high-security bank in Massachusetts in broad daylight by pretending that he and his men were guards making a routine pickup in an armored car. Tucker believed the plan was "a breakthrough in the art." On March 7th, moments before the armored car was scheduled to arrive, they put on makeup and mustaches; Tucker's wig had shrunk in a recent snowstorm, and rather than postpone the operation he decided to do without it.

The teller buzzed them in. Just as they were entering the vault, according to a police report, the manager noticed that "the dark mustache on one man and the white mustache on the other man were not real." One of the "guards" patted his gun and said, "This is a holdup."

Tucker locked the manager and two tellers inside the vault, and escaped with more than four hundred and thirty thousand dollars. But when the police showed the tellers a series of mug shots, they identified, for the first time, the leader of the Over-the-Hill Gang as the same man who had broken out of San Quentin in a homemade kayak three years earlier.

As the F.B.I., the local police, and the county sheriffs all tried to track him down, Tucker hid in Florida, checking in daily with Teddy Green, his old Alcatraz confidant. One June morning, Tucker pulled into Green's garage and waited while his friend walked toward the car. "I was looking at him," Tucker recalls, "thinking, My, what a sharp suit!"

A man jumped in front of Tucker's car and yelled, "F.B.I., don't move! You're under arrest."

Agents were everywhere, coming out of cars and bushes. Tucker glowered at Green, convinced that his friend had "ratted me out." Although Tucker insists that he never had a pistol—and none was ever found—several agents said they saw one in his hand. "He's got a gun!" one of them yelled, diving to the ground. The garage filled with the sound of gunfire. Bullets shattered the windshield and the radiator. Tucker, who had been hit in both arms and in the leg, ducked below the dashboard and pressed the accelerator, crashing outside the garage. He opened the car door and stumbled onto the street, his hands and face covered in blood. A woman with two children was driving toward him. "As I got closer," the woman later testified, "he started to look bloodier and bloodier—it was all over him—and I thought, This poor man has been hit by a car."

She offered him a ride, and he climbed into the passenger seat. Then, in her rearview mirror, she saw someone holding a rifle, and her six-year-old son cried out, "Criminal!" When she hesitated, Tucker grabbed the wheel and snapped, "I have a gun—now drive!" Her son began to sob. After a half-mile chase, they veered down a dead-end street. At a muttered "O.K." from Tucker, the woman scrambled out of the car and dragged her children to safety. Then Tucker himself stepped from the car and passed out.

A columnist for the *Miami Herald* summed up the capture of the longtime prison fugitive and leader of the Over-the-Hill Gang this way:

> There is something vaguely appealing about Tucker. . . . Old guys are not regularly associated with high crimes. . . . Tucker must also be admired, in a twisted way I admit, for pulling off an incredible escape from San Quentin prison in San Francisco. . . . Tucker might have made a fortune selling the escape yarn to Hollywood and holing up somewhere. Instead he chose to resume the line of work to which he was dedicated. . . . The aging Robin Hood took from the rich, who were probably loaded with insurance.

Tucker's story had, at last, acquired the burnish of outlaw mythology. The battered Rub-a-Dub-Dub had

been donated to the Marin Yacht Club and was later
placed in a prison museum, and the Children's Hospital Medical Center in Oakland requested that Tucker be
allowed to serve as grand marshal for its upcoming Bath-
tub Regatta. Amid the clamor, the F.B.I. showed up at
a fancy retirement community in Lauderhill, Florida,
where Tucker was believed to have been living. An ele-
gant woman in her fifties answered the door. When they
asked her about Forrest Tucker, she said she had never
heard of the man. She was married to Bob Callahan, a
successful stockbroker whom she had met shortly after
her first husband died. When the agents explained that
Bob Callahan was really Forrest Tucker, a man who had
broken out of jail four years earlier, she looked at them in
tears. "I told 'em, 'I don't believe a word you're saying,'"
she recalled, nearly two decades later. "But they had him.
They shot him three times."

An heiress to a modest moving-company fortune
who looked, in her youth, a bit like Marilyn Monroe, she
remembers meeting Tucker at the Whale and Porpoise,
a private club on Oakland Park Boulevard. She had never
encountered anyone so kind and gallant. "He came over
and asked me to dance, and that was that," she told me.

She recalled how she went to see him in prison ("still
in a daze"), not sure what to say or do. When she saw
him lying there, pale and bloodied, she was overcome
with love for this man who, she learned, had been in a

chain gang at sixteen. As he begged her forgiveness, she told me, "All I wanted to do was hold him."

At first, awaiting trial in Miami, Tucker tried to break out of jail, removing a bar in his cell with a hacksaw and climbing onto the roof with a homemade grappling hook. But after his wife promised—to the consternation of her family and friends—to stay with him if he reformed, Tucker vowed to rehabilitate himself. "I told her that from then on I'd only look at ways to escape," he says, adding, "She is one in a million."

He returned to San Quentin, where he was nicknamed "the captain," and where, for the first time, his seemingly impervious constitution began to show its age. In 1986, he underwent a quadruple bypass. Although guards stood by the door in case he tried to escape, he now considered himself strictly a legal contortionist. Years earlier, at Alcatraz, he had written an appeal that went all the way to the Supreme Court in which he successfully argued that a judge could not, at sentencing, take into account prior convictions received when the defendant lacked counsel. ("It is time we become just a little realistic in the face of a record such as this one," Justice Harry A. Blackmun wrote in an angry dissent.) Now, with his failing health, Tucker unleashed another flurry of appeals, getting his sentence reduced by more than half. "This is to thank you," he wrote one judge. "It's the first break I ever got in my life. I won't ever need another."

He began to pour all his energy into what he saw as the culmination of his life as an outlaw: a Hollywood movie. Tucker had seen all sorts of films that echoed his life, among them "I Am a Fugitive from a Chain Gang," "Escape from Alcatraz," and "Bonnie and Clyde," and he wanted, at last, to see his story enshrined in the American imagination. He began to put his exploits down on paper, five pages at a time. "No one could have written this inside story of the Rock and what really happened there unless they had personally lived it," he wrote. He devoted two hundred and sixty-one pages to "Alcatraz: The True Story," while working on a second, more ambitious account, which he titled "The Can Opener." In it, he described himself as a throwback "to the highly intelligent, nonviolent type of criminal in the Willie Sutton mold," and, more grandly, as a kind of heroic underdog, pitted against a vast and oppressive system. "Tucker's obsession with freedom and escape has transformed itself into gamesmanship," he wrote. "This is his way of keeping his sanity in a lifetime of being the hunted. Each new 'joint' is a game, a game to outwit the authorities."

In 1993, he was released, at the age of seventy-three, and settled into the peach-colored house in Pompano Beach, which his wife had bought for them. He polished his manuscript and set up a music room in the den, where he gave saxophone and clarinet lessons for twenty-five dollars an hour. "We had a wonderful life," his wife said.

Tucker recalls, "We used to go out dancing. She'd dress up real pretty, and I'd show her off." He composed music for her. "He has all these talents that had been wasted all these years," she told me. From time to time, he played in local jazz clubs. "I got used to being free," he says. But his manuscript failed to captivate people as he had hoped it would—"I called Clint Eastwood's secretary, but she said, 'Unless you have an agent, he won't read it'"—and the author of "The Can Opener" increasingly seemed trapped, an ordinary old man.

Then came the day in 1999 when, at the age of seventy-eight, he painted his fingertips with nail polish, pulled his white ascot up over his face, and burst into the Republic Security Bank with his gun. "He didn't do it for the money," his wife said. "We had a new car, nice home paid for, beautiful clothes. He had everything."

"I think he wanted to become a legend, like Bonnie and Clyde," said Captain Chinn, who apprehended him after what was believed to be his fourth recent robbery in the Florida area. A court psychologist who examined Tucker noted, "I have seen many individuals who are self-aggrandizing, and that would like to make their mark in history . . . but none, I must admit, that I heard that would want to, other than in the movies, go out in a blaze in a bank robbery. It is beyond the realm of psychological prediction."

After Tucker's arrest, the police put him in semi-isolation, fearing that even at seventy-eight he might somehow elude them. Despite his lawyer's pleas that his client could die under such conditions, he was denied bail. "Ordinarily, I would not consider a seventy-eight-year-old man a flight risk or a danger to the community," the magistrate said, "but Mr. Tucker has proved himself to be remarkably agile." On October 20, 2000, just before his case was scheduled to go to trial, and with his wife looking on, Tucker pleaded guilty. He was sentenced to thirteen years.

At one point, I found a report that the Department of Corrections had compiled, detailing Tucker's life. After pages listing his dramatic holdups and daredevil escapes, it concluded with a different kind of summary:

> The defendant does not know the whereabouts of [his] daughter. He stated he did not have an active part in this child's upbringing. . . . The defendant has no knowledge of his son's whereabouts. The defendant did not partake in the rearing of this child.

"I thought he died in an automobile accident," his son, Rick Bellew, told me over the phone after I tracked him down in Nevada, where he was living and working as a printer. "That's what my mom told me to protect me." He didn't know the truth, he said, until he was in his early twenties, when Tucker was about to be paroled. "My mom was afraid he'd come up to me on the street and freak me out."

He said that after his father was taken away the authorities confiscated all their furniture and possessions, which had been paid for with stolen cash. They had to move in with his grandparents, while his mother worked in a factory to support them. "He left us with nothing," he said. "He turned our world inside out."

After Bellew read about Tucker's last arrest, he wrote him a letter for the first time. "I needed to know why he did it," he said. "Why he sacrificed everything."

Although Tucker could never give him a satisfactory answer, they struck up a correspondence, and in one of his letters Tucker told him something he had never expected: Bellew had an older half sister named Gaile Tucker, a nurse who lived in Florida. "I called her up and said, 'Are you sitting down?' I said, 'This is your long-lost brother.' She said, 'Oh, my God.'" Later, the two met, studying each other's features for similarities, trying to piece together a portrait of a man they barely knew.

"I don't have any ill feelings," his daughter told me. "I just don't have any feelings."

At one point, Bellew read me part of a letter that Tucker had recently sent him: "I'm sorry things turned out the way they did. . . . I never got to take you fishing, or to baseball games or to see you grow up. . . . I don't ask you to forgive me as there is too much lost but just so you know I wish you the best. Always. Your dad, Forrest."

Bellew said he didn't know if he would continue the correspondence, not because of what Tucker had done to him but because of what he had done to his mother. "He blew my mother's world apart," Bellew told me. "She never remarried. There was a song she used to sing to me called 'Me and My Shadow,' all about being alone and blue. And when she had cancer, and wasn't going to live much longer, I broke down and she sang that song, and I realized how bittersweet it was. It was her life."

In the spring of 2002, when I visited Tucker's third wife in Pompano Beach, she seemed to be still trying to cope. A small, delicate woman, now in her seventies, she had had several operations and lived alone in their house. "With Forrest gone, there's no one to fix things up," she said. She paused, scanning the den where he used to keep his musical instruments. "The silence is unbearable." She showed me a picture of the two of them, taken shortly after they met. They are standing side by side, their arms touching. He has on a red shirt and tie, and his wavy hair is neatly combed to one side. "God, he used to be so handsome," she said. "When I met him, he was a *doll*."

She turned the picture of him over several times in her hand. "I waited all those years," she said as she walked me outside, wiping her eyes. "I thought we had the rest of our lives together. What am I supposed to do now?"

One of the last times I met Tucker in prison, he looked alarmingly frail. His facial muscles seemed slack, and his hands trembled. Since his incarceration, he had had several strokes, and a cardiologist concluded that blood clots were gradually cutting off oxygen to his brain. His daughter told me bluntly, "He'll die in prison."

"Everyone says I'm smart," Tucker said to me. "But I'm not smart in the ways of life or I wouldn't have done the things I did." After a brief flurry of attention following his arrest, he had been all but forgotten. "When I die, no one will remember me," he said. His voice was almost a whisper. "I wish I had a real profession, something like the music business. I regret not being able to work steady and support my family. I have other regrets, too, but that's as much as one man can stand. Late at night, you lie in your bunk in prison and you think about what you lost, what you were, what you could've been, and you regret."

He said that his wife was thinking of selling their house and moving into a community where she could see more people. Although he and his wife still spoke regularly, Tucker said, she was too frail to visit.

"What hurts most . . . is that I know how much I disappointed my wife," he went on. "That hurts more than anything."

As he rose to go, he took a piece of paper from his back pocket. "I made this up for you last night," he said.

On it was a list of all his escapes, neatly printed. At the bottom, there was a No. 19—one more than he had actually made—left blank. As the guard fetched his wheelchair, he waved him away. "I don't need my chariot," he said. Then slowly, with his back hunched, he steadied himself against the wall and, with the guard standing behind him, inched down the corridor.

—January, 2003

True Crime

**A POSTMODERN
MURDER MYSTERY**

In the southwest corner of Poland, far from any town or city, the Oder River curls sharply, creating a tiny inlet. The banks are matted with wild grass and shrouded by towering pine and oak trees. The only people who regularly trek to the area are fishermen—the inlet teems with perch and pike and sun bass. On a cold December day in 2000, three friends were casting there when one of them noticed something floating by the shore. At first, he thought it was a log, but as he drew closer he saw what looked like hair. The fisherman shouted to one of his friends, who poked the object with his rod. It was a dead body.

The fishermen called the police, who carefully removed the corpse of a man from the water. A noose was around his neck, and his hands were bound behind his back. Part of the rope, which appeared to have been cut with a knife, had once connected his hands to his neck, binding the man in a backward cradle, an excruciating position—the slightest wiggle would have caused the noose to tighten further. There was no doubt that the man had been murdered. His body was clothed in only a sweatshirt and underwear, and it bore marks of torture. A pathologist determined that the victim had virtually no food in his intestines, which indicated that he had been starved for several days before he was killed. Initially, the police thought that he had been strangled and then dumped in the river, but an examination of fluids in his lungs revealed signs of drowning, which meant that he was probably still alive when he was dropped into the water.

The victim—tall, with long dark hair and blue eyes—seemed to match the description of a thirty-five-year-old businessman named Dariusz Janiszewski, who had lived in the city of Wroclaw, sixty miles away, and who had been reported missing by his wife nearly four weeks earlier; he had last been seen on November 13th, leaving the small advertising firm that he owned, in downtown Wroclaw. When the police summoned Janiszewski's wife to see if she could identify the body, she was too distraught to look, and so Janiszewski's mother did instead. She immediately recognized her son's flowing hair and the birthmark on his chest.

The police launched a major investigation. Scuba

divers plunged into the frigid river, looking for evidence. Forensic specialists combed the forest. Dozens of associates were questioned, and Janiszewski's business records were examined. Nothing of note was found. Although Janiszewski and his wife, who had wed eight years earlier, had a brief period of trouble in their marriage, they had since reconciled and were about to adopt a child. He had no apparent debts or enemies, and no criminal record. Witnesses described him as a gentle man, an amateur guitarist who composed music for his rock band. "He was not the kind of person who would provoke fights," his wife said. "He wouldn't harm anybody."

After six months, the investigation was dropped, because of "an inability to find the perpetrator or perpetrators," as the prosecutor put it in his report. Janiszewski's family hung a cross on an oak tree near where the body was found—one of the few reminders of what the Polish press dubbed "the perfect crime."

One afternoon in the fall of 2003, Jacek Wroblewski, a thirty-eight-year-old detective in the Wroclaw police department, unlocked the safe in his office, where he stored his files, and removed a folder marked "Janiszewski." It was getting late, and most members of the department would soon be heading home, their thick wooden doors clapping shut, one after the other, in the long stone corridor of the fortress-like building, which the Germans had built in the early twentieth century, when Wroclaw was still part of Germany. (The building has underground tunnels leading to the jail and the courthouse, across the street.) Wroblewski, who preferred to work late at night, kept by his desk a coffee-pot and a small refrigerator; that was about all he could squeeze into the cell-like room, which was decorated with wall-sized maps of Poland and with calendars of scantily clad women, which he took down when he had official visitors.

The Janiszewski case was three years old, and had been handed over to Wroblewski's unit by the local police who had conducted the original investigation. The unsolved murder was the coldest of cold cases, and Wroblewski was drawn to it. He was a tall, lumbering man with a pink, fleshy face and a burgeoning paunch. He wore ordinary slacks and a shirt to work, instead of a uniform, and there was a simplicity to his appearance, which he used to his advantage: people trusted him because they thought that they had no reason to fear him. Even his superiors joked that his cases must somehow solve themselves. "Jacek" is "Jack" in English, and *wróbel* means "sparrow," and so his colleagues called him Jack Sparrow—the name of the Johnny Depp character in "Pirates of the Caribbean." Wroblewski liked to say in response, "I'm more of an eagle."

After Wroblewski graduated from high school, in 1984, he began searching for his "purpose in life," as he put it, working variously as a municipal clerk, a locksmith, a soldier, an aircraft mechanic, and, in defiance of the Communist government, a union organizer allied with Solidarity. In 1994, five years after the Communist regime collapsed, he joined the newly refashioned police force. Salaries for police officers in Poland were, and remain, dismal—a rookie earns only a few thousand dollars a year—and Wroblewski had a wife and two children to support. Still, he had finally found a position that suited him. A man with a stark Catholic vision of good and evil, he relished chasing criminals, and after putting away his first murderer he hung a pair of goat horns on his office wall, to symbolize the capture of his prey. During his few free hours, he studied psychology at a local university: he wanted to understand the criminal mind.

Wroblewski had heard about the murder of Janiszewski, but he was unfamiliar with the details, and he sat down at his desk to review the file. He knew that, in cold cases, the key to solving the crime is often an overlooked clue buried in the original file. He studied the pathologist's report and the photographs of the crime scene. The level of brutality, Wroblewski thought, suggested that the perpetrator, or perpetrators, had a deep grievance against Janiszewski. Moreover, the virtual absence of clothing on Janiszewski's battered body indicated that he had been stripped, in an attempt to humiliate him. (There was no evidence of sexual abuse.) According to Janiszewski's wife, her husband always carried credit cards, but they had not been used after the crime—another indication that this was no mere robbery.

Wroblewski read the various statements that had been given to the local police. The most revealing was from Janiszewski's mother, who had worked as a book-keeper in his advertising firm. On the day that her son disappeared, she stated, a man had called the office at around 9:30 A.M., looking for him. The caller made an urgent request. "Could you make three signs, quite big ones, and the third one as big as a billboard?" he asked. When she inquired further, he said, "I will not talk to you about this," demanding again to speak to her son. She explained that he was out of the office, but she gave the caller Janiszewski's cell-phone number. The man hung up. He had not identified himself, and Janiszewski's mother had not recognized his voice, though she thought that he sounded "professional." During the conversation, she had heard noise in the background, a dull roar. Later, when her son showed up at the office, she asked him if the customer had called, and Janiszewski replied that they had arranged to meet that afternoon. According to a receptionist in the building, who was the last known person to see Janiszewski alive, he departed the office at around four o'clock. He left his car, a Peugeot, in the parking lot, which his family said was very unusual: although he often met with customers away from the office, he habitually took his car.

Investigators, upon checking phone records, discovered that the call to Janiszewski's office had come from a phone booth down the street—this explained the background noise, Wroblewski thought. Records also indicated that, less than a minute after the call ended, someone at the same public phone had rung Janiszewski's cell phone. Though the calls were suspicious, Wroblewski could not be certain that the caller was a perpetrator, just as he could not yet say how many assailants were involved in the crime. Janiszewski was more than six feet tall and weighed some two hundred pounds, and tying him up and disposing of his body may have required accomplices. The receptionist reported that when Janiszewski left the office she had seen two men seemingly trailing him, though she could not describe them in any detail. Whoever was behind the abduction, Wroblewski thought, had been extremely organized and shrewd. The mastermind—Wroblewski assumed it was a man, based on the caller's voice—must have studied Janiszewski's business routine and known how to lure him out of his office and, possibly, into a car.

Wroblewski pored over the materials, trying to find something more, yet he remained stymied. After several hours, he locked the file in his safe, but over the next several days and nights he took it out again and again. At one point, he realized that Janiszewski's cell phone had never been found. Wroblewski decided to see if the phone could be traced—an unlikely possibility. Poland lagged behind other European countries in technological development, and its financially strapped police force was only beginning to adopt more sophisticated methods of tracking cellular and computer communications. Nevertheless, Wroblewski had taken a keen interest in these new techniques, and he began an elaborate search, with the help of the department's recently hired telecommunications specialist. Although Janiszewski's telephone number had not been used since his disappearance, Wroblewski knew that cell phones often bear a serial number from the manufacturer, and his men contacted Janiszewski's wife, who provided a receipt containing this information. To Wroblewski's astonishment, he and his colleague soon found a match: a cell phone with the same serial number had been sold on Allegro, an Internet auction site, four days after Janiszewski disappeared. The seller had logged in as ChrisB[7], who, investigators learned, was a thirty-year-old Polish intellectual named Krystian Bala.

It seemed inconceivable that a murderer who had orchestrated such a well-planned crime would have sold the victim's cell phone on an Internet auction site. Bala, Wroblewski realized, could have obtained it from someone else, or purchased it at a pawnshop, or even found it on the street. Bala had since moved abroad, and could not be easily reached, but as Wroblewski checked into his background he discovered that he had recently published a novel called "Amok." Wroblewski obtained a copy, which had on the cover a surreal image of a goat— an ancient symbol of the Devil. Like the works of the French novelist Michel Houellebecq, the book is sadistic, pornographic, and creepy. The main character, who narrates the story, is a bored Polish intellectual who, when not musing about philosophy, is drinking and having sex with women.

Wroblewski, who read mostly history books, was shocked by the novel's contents, which were not only decadent but vehemently anti-Church. He made note of the fact that the narrator murders a female lover for no reason ("What had come over me? What the hell did I do?") and conceals the act so well that he is never caught. Wroblewski was struck, in particular, by the killer's method: "I tightened the noose around her neck." Wroblewski then noticed something else: the killer's name is Chris, the English version of the author's first name. It was also the name that Krystian Bala had posted on the Internet auction site. Wroblewski began to read the book more closely—a hardened cop turned literary detective.

———

F̲our years earlier, in the spring of 1999, Krystian
Bala sat in a café in Wroclaw, wearing a three-piece
suit. He was going to be filmed for a documentary called
"Young Money," about the new generation of businessmen in the suddenly freewheeling Polish capitalist system. Bala, who was then twenty-six, had been chosen
for the documentary because he had started an industrial
cleaning business that used advanced machinery from
the United States. Though Bala had dressed up for the
occasion, he looked more like a brooding poet than like
a businessman. He had dark, ruminative eyes and thick
curly brown hair. Slender and sensitive-looking, he was
so handsome that his friends had nicknamed him Amour.
He chain-smoked and spoke like a professor of philosophy, which is what he had trained, and still hoped, to
become. "I don't feel like a businessman," Bala later told
the interviewer, adding that he had always "dreamed of
an academic career."

He had been the equivalent of high-school vale-
dictorian and, as an undergraduate at the University of
Wroclaw, which he attended from 1992 to 1997, he was
considered one of the brightest philosophy students. The
night before an exam, while other students were cram-
ming, he often stayed out drinking and carousing, only
to show up the next morning, dishevelled and hung over,
and score the highest marks. "One time, I went out with
him and nearly died taking the exam," his close friend

and former classmate Lotar Rasinski, who now teaches philosophy at another university in Wroclaw, recalls. Beata Sierocka, who was one of Bala's philosophy professors, says that he had a voracious appetite for learning and an "inquisitive, rebellious mind."

Bala, who often stayed with his parents in Chojnow, a provincial town outside Wroclaw, began bringing home stacks of philosophy books, lining the hallways and filling the basement. Poland's philosophy departments had long been dominated by Marxism, which, like liberalism, is rooted in Enlightenment notions of reason and in the pursuit of universal truths. Bala, however, was drawn to the radical arguments of Ludwig Wittgenstein, who maintained that language, like a game of chess, is essentially a social activity. Bala often referred to Wittgenstein as "my master." He also seized on Friedrich Nietzsche's notorious contention that "there are no facts, only interpretations" and that "truths are illusions which we have forgotten are illusions."

For Bala, such subversive ideas made particular sense after the collapse of the Soviet Empire, where language and facts had been wildly manipulated to create a false sense of history. "The end of Communism marked the death of one of the great meta-narratives," Bala later told me, paraphrasing the postmodernist Jean-François Lyotard. Bala once wrote in an e-mail to a friend, "Read Wittgenstein and Nietzsche! Twenty times each!"

Bala's father, Stanislaw, who was a construction worker and a taxi-driver ("I'm a simple, uneducated man," he says), was proud of his son's academic accomplishments. Still, he occasionally wanted to throw away Krystian's books and force him to "plant with me in the garden." Stanislaw sometimes worked in France, and during the summer Krystian frequently went with him to earn extra money for his studies. "He would bring suitcases stuffed with books," Stanislaw recalls. "He would work all day and study through the night. I used to joke that he knew more about France from books than from seeing it."

By then, Bala had become entranced by French postmodernists such as Jacques Derrida and Michel Foucault. He was particularly interested in Derrida's notion that not only is language too unstable to pinpoint any absolute truth; human identity itself is the malleable product of language. Bala wrote a thesis about Richard Rorty, the American philosopher, who famously declared, "The guise of convincing your peers is the very face of truth itself."

Bala interpreted these thinkers idiosyncratically, pulling threads here and there, and often twisting and turning and distorting them, until he had braided them into his own radical philosophy. To amuse himself, he began constructing myths about himself—an adventure in Paris, a romance with a schoolmate—and tried to convince friends that they were true. "He would tell these tall stories about himself," Rasinski says. "If he told one person, and that person then told someone else, who told someone else, it became true. It existed in the language." Rasinski adds, "Krystian even had a term for it. He called it 'mytho-creativity.'" Before long, friends had trouble distinguishing his real character from the one he had invented. In an e-mail to a friend, Bala said, "If I ever write an autobiography, it will be full of myths!"

Bala cast himself as an enfant terrible who sought out what Foucault had called a "limit-experience": he wanted to push the boundaries of language and human existence, to break free of what he deemed to be the hypocritical and oppressive "truths" of Western society, including taboos on sex and drugs. Foucault himself was drawn to homosexual sadomasochism. Bala devoured the works of Georges Bataille, who vowed to "brutally oppose all systems," and once contemplated carrying out human sacrifices; and William Burroughs, who swore to use language to "rub out the word"; and the Marquis de Sade, who demanded, "O man! Is it for you to say what is good or what is evil?" Bala boasted about his drunken visits to brothels and his submission to temptations of the flesh. He told friends that he hated "conventions" and was "capable of anything," and he insisted, "I will not live long but I will live furiously!"

Some people found such proclamations juvenile, even

ridiculous; others were mesmerized by them. "There were legends that no woman could resist him," one friend recalled. Those closest to him regarded his tales simply as playful confabulations. Sierocka, his former professor, says that Bala, in reality, was always "kind, energetic, hardworking, and principled." His friend Rasinski says, "Krystian liked the idea of being this Nietzschean superman, but anyone who knew him well realized that, as with his language games, he was just playing around."

In 1995, Bala, belying his libertine posture, married his high-school sweetheart, Stanislawa—or Stasia, as he called her. Stasia, who had dropped out of high school and worked as a secretary, showed little interest in language or philosophy. Bala's mother opposed the marriage, believing Stasia was ill-suited for her son. "I thought he should at least wait until he had finished his studies," she says. But Bala insisted that he wanted to take care of Stasia, who had always loved him, and in 1997 their son Kacper was born. That year, Bala graduated from the university with the highest possible marks, and enrolled in its Ph.D. program in philosophy. Although he received a full academic scholarship, he struggled to support his family, and soon left school to open his cleaning business. In the documentary on Poland's new generation of businessmen, Bala says, "Reality came and kicked me in the ass." With an air of resignation, he continues, "Once, I planned to paint graffiti on walls. Now I'm trying to wash it off."

He was not a good businessman. Whenever money came in, colleagues say, instead of investing it in his company he spent it. By 2000, he had filed for bankruptcy. His marriage also collapsed. "The basic problem was women," his wife later said. "I knew that he was having an affair." After Stasia separated from him, he seemed despondent and left Poland, travelling to the United States, and later to Asia, where he taught English and scuba diving.

He began to work intensively on "Amok," which encapsulated all his philosophical obsessions. The story mirrors "Crime and Punishment," in which Raskolnikov, convinced that he is a superior being who can deliver his own form of justice, murders a wretched pawnbroker. "Wouldn't thousands of good deeds make up for one tiny little crime?" Raskolnikov asks. If Raskolnikov is a Frankenstein's monster of modernity, then Chris, the protagonist of "Amok," is a monster of postmodernity. In his view, not only is there no sacred being ("God, if you only existed, you'd see how sperm looks on blood"); there is also no truth ("Truth is being displaced by narrative"). One character admits that he doesn't know which of his constructed personalities is real, and Chris says, "I'm a good liar, because I believe in the lies myself."

Unbound by any sense of truth—moral, scientific, historical, biographical, legal—Chris embarks on a grisly rampage. After his wife catches him having sex with her best friend and leaves him (Chris says that he has, at least, "stripped her of her illusions"), he sleeps with one woman after another, the sex ranging from numbing to sadomasochistic. Inverting convention, he lusts after ugly women, insisting that they are "more real, more touchable, more alive." He drinks too much. He spews vulgarities, determined, as one character puts it, to pulverize the language, to "screw it like no one else has ever screwed it." He mocks traditional philosophers and blasphemes the Catholic Church. In one scene, he gets drunk with a friend and steals from a church a statue of St. Anthony—the Egyptian saint who lived secluded in the desert, battling the temptations of the Devil, and who fascinated Foucault. (Foucault, describing how St. Anthony had turned to the Bible to ward off the Devil, only to encounter a bloody description of Jews slaughtering their enemies, writes that "evil is not embodied in individuals" but "incorporated in words" and that even a book of salvation can open "the gates to Hell.")

Finally, Chris, repudiating what is considered the ultimate moral truth, kills his girlfriend Mary. "I tightened the noose around her neck, holding her down with one hand," he says. "With my other hand, I stabbed the knife below her left breast. . . . Everything was covered in blood." He then ejaculates on her. In a perverse echo of Wittgenstein's notion that some actions defy language, Chris says of the killing, "There was no noise, no words, no movement. Complete silence."

In "Crime and Punishment," Raskolnikov confesses his sins and is punished for them, while being redeemed by the love of a woman named Sonya, who helps to guide him back toward a pre-modern Christian order. But Chris never removes what he calls his "white gloves of silence," and he is never punished. ("Murder leaves no stain," he declares.) And his wife—who, not coincidentally, is also named Sonya—never returns to him.

The style and structure of "Amok," which is derivative of many postmodern novels, reinforces the idea that truth is illusory—what is a novel, anyway, but a lie, a mytho-creation? Bala's narrator often addresses the reader, reminding him that he is being seduced by a work of fiction. "I am starting my story," Chris says. "I must avoid boring you." In another typical flourish, Chris reveals that he is reading a book about the violent rebellion of a young author with a "guilty conscience"— in other words, the same story as "Amok."

Throughout the book, Bala plays with words in order to emphasize their slipperiness. The title of one chapter, "Screwdriver," refers simultaneously to the tool, the cocktail, and Chris's sexual behavior. Even when Chris slaughters Mary, it feels like a language game. "I pulled the knife and rope from underneath the bed, as if I were about to begin a children's fairy tale," Chris says. "Then I started unwinding this fable of rope, and to make it more interesting I started to make a noose. It took me two million years."

Bala finished the book toward the end of 2002. He had given Chris a biography similar to his own, blurring the boundary between author and narrator. He even posted sections of the book on a blog called Amok, and during discussions with readers he wrote comments under the name Chris, as if he were the character. After the book came out, in 2003, an interviewer asked him, "Some authors write only to release their . . . Mr. Hyde, the dark side of their psyche—do you agree?" Bala joked in response, "I know what you are driving at, but I won't comment. It might turn out that Krystian Bala is the creation of Chris . . . not the other way around."

Few bookstores in Poland carried "Amok," in part because of the novel's shocking content, and those which did placed it on the highest shelves, out of the reach of children. (The book has not been translated into English.) On the Internet, a couple of reviewers praised "Amok." "We haven't had this kind of book in Polish literature," one wrote, adding that it was "paralyzingly realistic, totally vulgar, full of paranoid and delirious images." Another called it a "masterpiece of illusion." Yet most readers considered the book, as one major Polish newspaper put it, to be "without literary merit." Even one of Bala's friends dismissed it as "rubbish." When Sierocka, the philosophy professor, opened it, she was stunned by its crude language, which was the antithesis of the straightforward, intelligent style of the papers that

Bala had written at the university. "Frankly, I found the book hard to read," she says. An ex-girlfriend of Bala's later said, "I was shocked by the book, because he never used those words. He never acted obscenely or vulgar toward me. Our sex life was normal."

Many of Bala's friends believed that he wanted to do in his fiction what he never did in life: shatter every taboo. In the interview that Bala gave after "Amok" was published, he said, "I wrote the book not caring about any convention. . . . A simple reader will find interesting only a few violent scenes with a graphic description of people having sex. But if someone really looks, he will see that these scenes are intended to awaken the reader and . . . show how fucked up and impoverished and hypocritical this world is."

By Bala's own estimate, "Amok" sold only a couple of thousand copies. But he was confident that it would eventually find its place among the great works of literature. "I'm truly convinced that one day my book will be appreciated," he said. "History teaches that some works of art have to wait ages before they are recognized."

In at least one respect, the book succeeded. Chris was so authentically creepy that it was hard not to believe that he was the product of a genuinely disturbed mind, and that he and the author were indeed indistinguishable. On Bala's Web site, readers described him and his work as "grotesque," "sexist," and "psychopathic." During an Internet conversation, in June of 2003, a friend told Bala that his book did not give the reader a good impression of him. When Bala assured her that the book was fiction, she insisted that Chris's musings had to be "your thoughts." Bala became irritated. Only a fool, he said, would believe that.

Detective Wroblewski underlined various passages as he studied "Amok." At first glance, few details of Mary's murder resembled the killing of Janiszewski. Most conspicuously, the victim in the novel is a woman, and the killer's longtime friend. Moreover, although Mary has a noose around her neck, she gets stabbed, with a Japanese knife, and Janiszewski wasn't. One detail in the book, however, chilled Wroblewski: after the murder, Chris says, "I sell the Japanese knife on an Internet auction." The similarity to the selling of Janiszewski's cell phone on the Internet—a detail that the police had never released to the public—seemed too extraordinary to be a coincidence.

At one point in "Amok," Chris intimates that he has also killed a man. When one of his girlfriends doubts his endless mytho-creations, he says, "Which story didn't you believe—that my radio station went bankrupt or that I killed a man who behaved inappropriately toward me ten years ago?" He adds of the murder, "Everyone con-

siders it a fable. Maybe it's better that way. Fuck. Sometimes I don't believe it myself."

Wroblewski had never read about postmodernism
or language games. For him, facts were as indissoluble
as bullets. You either killed someone or you didn't. His
job was to piece together a logical chain of evidence
that revealed the irrefutable truth. But Wroblewski
also believed that, in order to catch a killer, you had to
understand the social and psychological forces that had
formed him. And so, if Bala had murdered Janiszewski
or participated in the crime—as Wroblewski now fully
suspected—then Wroblewski, the empiricist, would have
to become a postmodernist.

To the surprise of members of his detective squad,
Wroblewski made copies of the novel and handed them
out. Everyone was assigned a chapter to "interpret": to
try to find any clues, any coded messages, any parallels
with reality. Because Bala was living outside the country,
Wroblewski warned his colleagues not to do anything
that might alarm the author. Wroblewski knew that if
Bala did not voluntarily return home to see his family,
as he periodically did, it would be virtually impossible
for the Polish police to apprehend him. At least for
the moment, the police had to refrain from questioning Bala's family and friends. Instead, Wroblewski and
his team combed public records and interrogated Bala's
more distant associates, constructing a profile of the sus-

pect, which they then compared with the profile of Chris in the novel. Wroblewski kept an unofficial scorecard: both Bala and his literary creation were consumed by philosophy, had been abandoned by their wives, had a company go bankrupt, travelled around the world, and drank too much. Wroblewski discovered that Bala had once been detained by the police, and when he obtained the official report it was as if he had already read it. As Bala's friend Pawel, who was detained with him, later testified in court, "Krystian came to me in the evening and had a bottle with him. We started drinking. Actually, we drank till dawn." Pawel went on, "The alcohol ran out, so we went to a store to buy another bottle. As we were returning from the shop we passed by a church, and this is when we had a very stupid idea."

"What idea did you have?" the judge asked him.

"We went into the church and we saw St. Anthony's figure, and we took it."

"What for?" the judge inquired.

"Well, we wanted a third person to drink with. Krystian said afterward that we were crazy."

In the novel, when the police catch Chris and his friend drinking beside the statue of St. Anthony, Chris says, "We were threatened by prison! I was speechless. . . . I do not feel like a criminal, but I became one. I had done much worse things in my life, and never suffered any consequences."

Wroblewski began to describe "Amok" as a "road map" to a crime, but some authorities objected that he was pushing the investigation in a highly suspect direction. The police asked a criminal psychologist to analyze the character of Chris, in order to gain insight into Bala. The psychologist wrote in her report, "The character of Chris is an egocentric man with great intellectual ambitions. He perceives himself as an intellectual with his own philosophy, based on his education and high I.Q. His way of functioning shows features of psychopathic behavior. He is testing the limits to see if he can actually carry out his . . . sadistic fantasies. He treats people with disrespect, considers them to be intellectually inferior to himself, uses manipulation to fulfill his own needs, and is determined to satiate his sexual desires in a hedonistic way. If such a character were real—a true living person—his personality could have been shaped by a highly unrealistic sense of his own worth. It could also be . . . a result of psychological wounds and his insecurities as a man . . . pathological relationships with his parents or unacceptable homosexual tendencies." The psychologist acknowledged the links between Bala and Chris, such as divorce and philosophical interests, but cautioned that such overlaps were "common with novelists." And she warned, "Basing an analysis of the author on his fictional character would be a gross violation."

Wroblewski knew that details in the novel did not

qualify as evidence—they had to be corroborated independently. So far, though, he had only one piece of concrete evidence linking Bala to the victim: the cell phone. In February, 2002, the Polish television program "997," which, like "America's Most Wanted," solicits the public's help in solving crimes (997 is the emergency telephone number in Poland), aired a segment devoted to Janiszewski's murder. Afterward, the show posted on its Web site the latest news about the progress of the investigation, and asked for tips. Wroblewski and his men carefully analyzed the responses. Over the years, hundreds of people had visited the Web site, from places as far away as Japan, South Korea, and the United States. Yet the police didn't turn up a single fruitful lead.

When Wroblewski and the telecommunications expert checked to see if Bala had purchased or sold any other items on the Internet while logged on as ChrisB[7], they made a curious discovery. On October 17, 2000, a month before Janiszewski was kidnapped, Bala had clicked on the Allegro auction site for a police manual called "Accidental, Suicidal, or Criminal Hanging." "Hanging a mature, conscious, healthy, and physically fit person is very difficult even for several people," the manual stated, and described various ways that a noose might be tied. Bala did not purchase the book on Allegro, and it was unclear if he obtained it elsewhere, but the fact that he was seeking such information was, at least to Wroblewski, a sign of premeditation. Still, Wroblewski knew that if he wanted to convict Bala of murder he would need more than the circumstantial evidence he had gathered: he would need a confession.

Bala remained abroad, supporting himself by publishing articles in travel magazines, and by teaching English and scuba diving. In January of 2005, while visiting Micronesia, he sent an e-mail to a friend, saying, "I'm writing this letter from paradise."

Finally, that fall, Wroblewski learned that Bala was coming home.

"At approximately 2:30 P.M., after leaving a drugstore at Legnicka Street, in Chojnow, I was attacked by three men," Bala later wrote in a statement, describing what happened to him on September 5, 2005, shortly after he returned to his hometown. "One of them twisted my arms behind my back; another squeezed my throat so that I could not speak, and could barely breathe. Meanwhile, the third one handcuffed me."

Bala said that his attackers were tall and muscular, with close-cropped hair, like skinheads. Without telling Bala who they were or what they wanted, they forced him into a dark-green vehicle and slipped a black plastic bag over his head. "I couldn't see anything," Bala said. "They ordered me to lie facedown on the floor."

Bala said that his assailants continued to beat him, shouting, "You fucking prick! You motherfucker!" He pleaded with them to leave him alone and not hurt him. Then he heard one of the men say on a cell phone, "Hi, boss! We got the shithead! Yes, he's still alive. So now what? At the meeting point?" The man continued, "And what about the money? Will we get it today?"

Bala said he thought that, because he lived abroad and was known to be a writer, the men assumed that he was wealthy and were seeking a ransom. "I tried to explain to them that I didn't have money," Bala stated. The more he spoke, though, the more brutally they attacked him.

Eventually, the car came to a stop, apparently in a wooded area. "We can dig a hole for this shit here and bury him," one of the men said. Bala struggled to breathe through the plastic bag. "I thought that this was going to be the last moment of my life, but suddenly they got back into the car and began driving again," he said.

After a long time, the car came to another stop, and the men shoved him out of the car and into a building. "I didn't hear a door, but because there was no wind or sun I assumed that we had entered," Bala said. The men threatened to kill him if he didn't cooperate, then led him upstairs into a small room, where they stripped him, deprived him of food, beat him, and began to interrogate him. Only then, Bala said, did he realize that he was in police custody and had been brought in for questioning by a man called Jack Sparrow.

———

"None of it happened," Wroblewski later told me. "We used standard procedures and followed the letter of the law."

According to Wroblewski and other officers, they apprehended Bala by the drugstore without violence and drove him to police headquarters in Wroclaw. Wroblewski and Bala sat facing each other in the detective's cramped office; a lightbulb overhead cast a faint glow, and Bala could see on the wall the goat horns that eerily resembled the image on the cover of his book. Bala appeared gentle and scholarly, yet Wroblewski recalled how, in "Amok," Chris says, "It's easier for people to imagine that Christ can turn urine into beer than that someone like me can send to Hell some asshole smashed into a lump of ground meat."

Wroblewski initially circled around the subject of the murder, trying to elicit offhand information about Bala's business and his relationships, and concealing what the police already knew about the crime—an interrogator's chief advantage. When Wroblewski did confront him about the killing, Bala looked dumbfounded. "I didn't know Dariusz Janiszewski," he said. "I know nothing about the murder."

Wroblewski pressed him about the curious details in "Amok." Bala later told me, "It was insane. He treated the book as if it were my literal autobiography. He must have read the book a hundred times. He knew it by heart." When Wroblewski mentioned several "facts" in the novel, such as the theft of the statue of St. Anthony, Bala acknowledged that he had drawn certain elements from his life. As Bala put it to me, "Sure, I'm guilty of that. Show me an author who *doesn't* do that."

Wroblewski then played his trump card: the cell phone. How did Bala get hold of it? Bala said that he couldn't remember—it was five years ago. Then he said that he must have bought the phone at a pawnshop, as he had done several times in the past. He agreed to take a polygraph test.

Wroblewski helped to prepare the questions for the examiner, who asked:

Just before Dariusz Janiszewski lost his life, did you know this would happen?
Were you the one who killed him?
Do you know who actually murdered him?
Did you know Janiszewski?
Were you in the place where Janiszewski was held hostage?

Bala replied no to each question. Periodically, he seemed to slow his breathing, in the manner of a scuba diver. The examiner wondered if he was trying to manipulate the test. On some questions, the examiner suspected Bala of lying, but, overall, the results were inconclusive.

In Poland, after a suspect is detained for forty-eight hours, the prosecutor in the case is required to present his evidence before a judge and charge the suspect; otherwise, the police must release him. The case against Bala remained weak. All Wroblewski and the police had was the cell phone, which Bala could have obtained, as he claimed, from a pawnshop; the sketchy results of a polygraph, a notoriously unreliable test; a book on hanging that Bala might not even have purchased; and clues possibly embedded in a novel. Wroblewski had no motive or confession. As a result, the authorities charged Bala only with selling stolen property—Janiszewski's phone—and with paying a bribe in an unrelated business matter, which Wroblewski had uncovered during the course of his investigation. Wroblewski knew that neither charge would likely carry any jail time, and although Bala had to remain in the country and relinquish his passport, he was otherwise a free man. "I had spent two years trying to build a case, and I was watching it all collapse," Wroblewski recalled.

Later, as he was flipping through Bala's passport, Wroblewski noticed stamps from Japan, South Korea, and the United States. He remembered that the Web site of the television show "997" had recorded page views from all of those countries—a fact that had baffled inves-

tigators. Why would anyone so far away be interested in
a local Polish murder? Wroblewski compared the peri-
ods when Bala was in each country with the timing of
the page views. The dates matched.

Bala, meanwhile, was becoming a cause célèbre. As
Wroblewski continued to investigate him for murder,
Bala filed a formal grievance with the authorities, claiming that he had been kidnapped and tortured. When Bala
told his friend Rasinski that he was being persecuted for
his art, Rasinski was incredulous. "I figured that he was
testing out some crazy idea for his next novel," he recalls.
Soon after, Wroblewski questioned Rasinski about his
friend. "That's when I realized that Krystian was telling
the truth," Rasinski says.

Rasinski was shocked when Wroblewski began to
grill him about "Amok." "I told him that I recognized
some details from real life, but that, to me, the book was
a work of fiction," Rasinski says. "This was crazy. You
cannot prosecute a man based on the novel he wrote."
Beata Sierocka, Bala's former professor, who was also
called in for questioning, says that she felt as if she were
being interrogated by "literary theorists."

As outrage over the investigation mounted, one of
Bala's girlfriends, Denise Rinehart, set up a defense
committee on his behalf. Rinehart, an American theatre

director, met Bala while she was studying in Poland, in 2001, and they had subsequently travelled together to the United States and South Korea. Rinehart solicited support over the Internet, writing, "Krystian is the author of a fictional philosophical book called 'Amok.' A lot of the language and content is strong and there are several metaphors that might be considered against the Catholic Church and Polish tradition. During his brutal interrogation they referenced his book numerous times, citing it as proof of his guilt."

Dubbing the case the Sprawa Absurd—the Absurd Matter—the committee contacted human-rights organizations and International PEN. Before long, the Polish Justice Ministry was deluged with letters on Bala's behalf from around the world. One said, "Mr. Bala deserves his rights in accordance with Article 19 of the U.N. Declaration of Human Rights that guarantees the right to freedom of expression. . . . We urge you to insure there is an immediate and thorough investigation into his kidnapping and imprisonment and that all of those found responsible are brought to justice."

Bala, writing in imperfect English, sent out frantic bulletins to the defense committee, which published them in a newsletter. In a bulletin on September 13, 2005, Bala warned that he was being "spied" on and said, "I want you to know that I will fight until the end." The next day, he said of Wroblewski and the police, "They have ruined my family life. We will never talk loud at home again. We will never use Internet freely again. We will never make any phone calls not thinking about who is listening. My mother takes some pills to stay calm. Otherwise she would get insane, because of this absurd accusation. My old father smokes 50 cigs a day and I smoke three packs. We all sleep 3–4 hours daily and we are afraid of leaving a house. Every single bark of our little dog alerts us and we don't know what or who to expect. It's a terror! Quiet Terror!"

The Polish authorities, meanwhile, had launched an internal investigation into Bala's allegations of mistreatment. In early 2006, after months of probing, the investigators declared that they had found no corroborating evidence. In this instance, they insisted, Bala's tale was indeed a mytho-creation.

"I have infected you," Chris warns the reader at the beginning of "Amok." "You will not be able to get free of me." Wroblewski remained haunted by one riddle in the novel, which, he believed, was crucial to solving the case. A character asks Chris, "Who was the one-eyed man among the blind?" The phrase derives from Erasmus (1469–1536), the Dutch theologian and classical scholar, who said, "In the kingdom of the blind, the one-eyed man is king." Who in "Amok," Wroblewski wondered, was the one-eyed man? And who were the blind men? In the novel's last line, Chris suddenly claims that he has solved the riddle, explaining, "This was the one killed by blind jealousy." But the sentence, with its strange lack of context, made little sense.

One hypothesis based on "Amok" was that Bala had murdered Janiszewski after beginning a homosexual affair with him. In the novel, after Chris's closest friend confesses that he is gay, Chris says that part of him wanted to "strangle him with a rope" and "chop a hole in a frozen river and dump him there." Still, the theory seemed dubious. Wroblewski had thoroughly investigated Janiszewski's background and there was no indication that he was gay.

Another theory was that the murder was the culmination of Bala's twisted philosophy—that he was a postmodern version of Nathan Leopold and Richard Loeb, the two brilliant Chicago students who, in the nineteen-twenties, were so entranced by Nietzsche's ideas that they killed a fourteen-year-old boy to see if they could execute the perfect murder and become supermen. At their trial, in which they received life sentences, Clarence Darrow, the legendary defense attorney who represented them, said of Leopold, "Here is a boy at sixteen or seventeen becoming obsessed with these doctrines. It was not a casual bit of philosophy with him; it was his life." Darrow, trying to save the boys from the death penalty, concluded, "Is there any blame attached because somebody took Nietzsche's philosophy seriously and fashioned his life upon it? . . . It is hardly fair to hang a nineteen-year-old boy for the philosophy that was taught him at the university."

In "Amok," Chris clearly aspires to be a postmodern *Übermensch*, speaking of his "will to power" and insisting that anyone who is "unable to kill should not stay alive." Yet these sentiments did not fully explain the murder of the unknown man in the novel, who, Chris says, had "behaved inappropriately" toward him. Chris, alluding to what happened between them, says teasingly, "Maybe he didn't do anything significant, but the most vicious Devil is in the details." If Bala's philosophy had justified, in his mind, a break from moral constraints, including the prohibition on murder, these passages suggested that there was still another motive, a deep personal connection to the victim—something that the brutality of the crime also indicated. With Bala unable to leave Poland, Wroblewski and his team began to question the suspect's closest friends and family.

Many of those interrogated saw Bala positively—"a bright, interesting man," one of his former girlfriends said of him. Bala had recently received a reference from a past employer at an English-instruction school in Poland, which described him as "intelligent," "inquisitive," and "easy to get along with," and praised his "keen sense of humor." The reference concluded, "With no reservation, I highly recommend Krystian Bala for any teaching position with children."

Yet, as Wroblewski and his men deepened their search for the "Devil in the details," a darker picture of Bala's life began to emerge. The years 1999 and 2000, during which time his business and his marriage collapsed—and Janiszewski was murdered—had been especially troubled. A friend recalled that Bala once "started to behave vulgarly and wanted to take his clothes off and show his manliness." The family babysitter described him as increasingly drunk and out of control. She said he constantly berated his wife, Stasia, shouting at her that "she slept around and cheated on him."

According to several people, after Bala and his wife separated, in 2000, he remained possessive of her. A friend, who called Bala an "authoritarian type," said of him, "He continuously controlled Stasia, and checked her phones." At a New Year's Eve party in 2000, just weeks after Janiszewski's body was found, Bala thought a bartender was making advances toward his wife and, as one witness put it, "went crazy." Bala screamed that he would take care of the bartender and that he had "already dealt with such a guy." At the time, Stasia and her friends had dismissed his drunken outburst. Even so, it took five people to restrain Bala; as one of them told police, "He was running amok."

As Wroblewski and his men were trying to fix on a motive, other members of the squad stepped up their efforts to trace the two suspicious telephone calls that had been made to Janiszewski's office and to his cell phone on the day he disappeared. The public telephone from which both calls were made was operated with a card. Each card was embedded with a unique number that registered with the phone company whenever it was used. Not long after Bala was released, the telecommunications expert on the Janiszewski case was able to determine the number on the caller's card. Once the police had that information, officials could trace all the telephone numbers dialled with that same card. Over a three-month period, thirty-two calls had been made. They included calls to Bala's parents, his girlfriend, his friends, and a business associate. "The truth was becoming clearer and clearer," Wroblewski said.

Wroblewski and his team soon uncovered another connection between the victim and the suspect. Malgorzata Drozdzal, a friend of Stasia's, told the police that in the summer of 2000 she had gone with Stasia to a night club called Crazy Horse, in Wroclaw. While Drozdzal was dancing, she saw Stasia talking to a man with long hair and bright-blue eyes. She recognized him from around town. His name was Dariusz Janiszewski.

Wroblewski had one last person to question: Stasia. But she had steadfastly refused to cooperate. Perhaps she was afraid of her ex-husband. Perhaps she believed Bala's claim that he was being persecuted by the police. Or perhaps she dreaded the idea of one day telling her son that she had betrayed his father.

Wroblewski and his men approached Stasia again, this time showing her sections of "Amok," which was published after she and Bala had split up, and which she had never looked at closely. According to Polish authorities, Stasia examined passages involving Chris's wife, Sonya, and was so disturbed by the character's similarities to her that she finally agreed to talk.

She confirmed that she had met Janiszewski at Crazy Horse. "I had ordered French fries, and I asked a man next to the bar whether the French fries were ready," Stasia recalled. "That man was Dariusz." They spent the entire night talking, she said, and Janiszewski gave her his phone number. Later, they went on a date and checked into a motel. But before anything happened, she said, Janiszewski admitted that he was married, and she left. "Since I know what it's like to be a wife whose husband betrays her, I didn't want to do that to another woman," Stasia said. The difficulties in Janiszewski's marriage soon ended, and he and Stasia never went out together again.

Several weeks after her date with Janiszewski, Stasia said, Bala showed up at her place in a drunken fury, demanding that she admit to having an affair with Janiszewski. He broke down the front door and struck her. He shouted that he had hired a private detective and knew everything. "He also mentioned that he had visited Dariusz's office, and described it to me," Stasia recalled. "Then he said he knew which hotel we went to and what room we were in."

Later, when she learned that Janiszewski had disappeared, Stasia said, she asked Bala if he had anything to do with it, and he said no. She did not pursue the matter, believing that Bala, for all his tumultuous behavior, was incapable of murder.

For the first time, Wroblewski thought he understood the last line of "Amok": "This was the one killed by blind jealousy."

Spectators flooded into the courtroom in Wroclaw on February 22, 2007, the first day of Bala's trial. There were philosophers, who argued with each other over the consequences of postmodernism; young lawyers, who wanted to learn about the police department's new investigative techniques; and reporters, who chronicled every tantalizing detail. "Killing doesn't make much of an impression in the twenty-first century, but allegedly killing and then writing about it in a novel is front-page news," a front-page article in *Angora*, a weekly based in Lodz, declared.

The judge, Lydia Hojenska, sat at the head of the courtroom, beneath an emblem of the white Polish eagle. In accordance with Polish law, the presiding judge, along with another judge and three citizens, acted as the jury. The defense and the prosecution sat at two unadorned wooden tables; next to the prosecutors were Janiszewski's widow and his parents, his mother holding a picture of her son. The public congregated in the back of the room, and in the last row was a stout, nervous woman with short red hair, who looked as if her own life were at stake. It was Bala's mother, Teresa; his father was too distraught to attend.

Everyone's attention, it seemed, was directed toward a zoolike cage near the center of the courtroom. It was almost nine feet high and twenty feet long, and had thick metal bars. Standing in the middle of it, wearing a suit and peering out calmly through his spectacles, was Krystian Bala. He faced up to twenty-five years in prison.

A trial is predicated on the idea that truth is obtainable. Yet it is also, as the writer Janet Malcolm has noted, a struggle between "two competing narratives," and "the story that can best withstand the attrition of the rules of evidence is the story that wins." In this case, the prosecution's narrative resembled that of "Amok": Bala, like his alter ego Chris, was a depraved hedonist, who, unbound by any sense of moral compunction, had murdered someone in a fit of jealous rage. The prosecution introduced files from Bala's computer, which Wroblewski and the police had seized during a raid of his parents' house. In one file, which had to be accessed with the password "amok," Bala catalogued, in graphic detail, sexual encounters with more than seventy women. The list included his wife, Stasia; a divorced cousin, who was "older" and "plump"; the mother of a friend, described as "old ass, hard-core action"; and a Russian "whore in an old car." The prosecution also presented e-mails in which Bala sounded unmistakably like Chris, using the same vulgar or arcane words, such as "joy juices" and "Madame Melancholy." In an angry e-mail to Stasia, Bala wrote, "Life is not only screwing, darling"—which echoed Chris's exclamation "Fucking is not the end of the world, Mary." A psychologist testified that "every author puts some part of his personality into his artistic creation," and that Chris and the defendant shared "sadistic" qualities.

During all this, Bala sat in the cage, taking notes on the proceedings or looking curiously out at the crowd. At times, he seemed to call into question the premise that the truth can be discerned. Under Polish law, the defendant can ask questions directly of the witnesses, and Bala eagerly did so, his professorial inquiries often phrased to reveal the Derridean instability of their testimony. When a former girlfriend testified that Bala once went out on her balcony drunk and acted as if he were on the verge of committing suicide, he asked her if her words might have multiple interpretations. "Could we just say that this is a matter of semantics—a misuse of the word 'suicide'?" he said.

But, as the trial wore on and the evidence mounted against him, the postmodernist sounded increasingly like an empiricist, a man desperately looking to show gaps in the prosecution's chain of evidence. Bala noted that no one had seen him kidnap Janiszewski, or kill him, or dump his body. "I'd like to say that I never met Dariusz, and there is not a single witness who would confirm that I did so," Bala said. He complained that the prosecution was taking random incidents in his personal life and weaving them into a story that no longer resembled reality. The prosecutors were constructing a mythocreation—or, as Bala's defense attorney put it to me, "the plot of a novel." According to the defense, the police and the media had been seduced by the most alluring story rather than by the truth. (Stories about the case had appeared under headlines such as "TRUTH STRANGER THAN FICTION" and "MURDER, HE WROTE.")

Bala had long subscribed to the postmodernist notion of "the death of the author"—that an author has no more access to the meaning of his literary work than anyone else. Yet, as the prosecution presented to the jury potentially incriminating details from "Amok," Bala complained that his novel was being misinterpreted. He insisted that the murder of Mary was simply a symbol of the "destruction of philosophy," and he made one last attempt to assert authorial control. As he later put it to me, "I'm the fucking author! I know what I meant."

In early September, the case went to the jury. Bala never took the stand, but in a statement he said, "I do believe the court will make the right decision and absolve me of all the charges." Wroblewski, who had been promoted to inspector, showed up in court, hoping to hear the verdict. "Even when you're sure of the facts, you wonder if someone else will see them the same way you do," he told me.

At last, the judges and jurors filed back into the courtroom. Bala's mother waited anxiously. She had never read "Amok," which contains a scene of Chris fantasizing about raping his mother. "I started to read the book, but it was too hard," she told me. "If someone else had written the book, maybe I would have read it, but I'm his mother." Bala's father appeared in the courtroom for the first time. He had read the novel, and though he had trouble understanding parts of it, he thought it was an important work of literature. "You can read it ten, twenty times, and each time discover something new in it," he said. On his copy, Bala had written an inscription to both his parents. It said, "Thank you for your . . . forgiveness of all my sins."

As Judge Hojenska read the verdict, Bala stood per-

fectly straight and still. Then came the one unmistakable
word: "Guilty."

The gray cinder-block prison in Wroclaw looks
like a relic of the Soviet era. After I slipped my visitor's pass through a tiny hole in the wall, a disembodied
voice ordered me to the front of the building, where a
solid gate swung open and a guard emerged, blinking
in the sunlight. The guard waved me inside as the gate
slammed shut behind us. After being searched, I was led
through several dank interlocking chambers and into a
small visitors' room with dingy wooden tables and chairs.
Conditions in Polish prisons are notorious. Because of
overcrowding, as many as seven people are often kept in
a single cell. In 2004, prison inmates in Wroclaw staged
a three-day hunger strike to protest overcrowding, poor
food, and insufficient medical care. Violence is also a
problem: only a few days before I arrived, I was told, a
visitor had been stabbed to death by an inmate.

In the corner of the visitors' room was a slender,
handsome man with wire-rimmed glasses and a navy-
blue artist's smock over a T-shirt that said "University of
Wisconsin." He was holding a book and looked like an
American student abroad, and it took me a moment to
realize that I was staring at Krystian Bala. "I'm glad you
could come," he said as he shook my hand, leading me to

one of the tables. "This whole thing is farce, like something out of Kafka." He spoke clear English but with a heavy accent, so that his "s"es sounded like "z"s.

Sitting down, he leaned across the table, and I could see that his cheeks were drawn, he had dark circles around his eyes, and his curly hair was standing up in front, as if he had been anxiously running his fingers through it. "I am being sentenced to prison for twenty-five years for writing a book—a book!" he said. "It is ridiculous. It is bullshit. Excuse my language, but that is what it is. Look, I wrote a novel, a crazy novel. Is the book vulgar? Yes. Is it obscene? Yes. Is it bawdy? Yes. Is it offensive? Yes. I intended it to be. This was a work of provocation." He paused, searching for an example, then added, "I wrote, for instance, that it would be easier for Christ to come out of a woman's womb than for me—" He stopped, catching himself. "I mean, for the narrator to fuck her. You see, this is *supposed* to offend." He went on, "What is happening to me is like what happened to Salman Rushdie."

As he spoke, he placed the book that he was carrying on the table. It was a worn, battered copy of "Amok." When I asked Bala about the evidence against him, such as the cell phone and the calling card, he sounded evasive and, at times, conspiratorial. "The calling card is not mine," he said. "Someone is trying to set me up. I don't know who yet, but someone is out to destroy me." His hand touched mine. "Don't you see what they are doing? They are constructing this reality and forcing me to live inside it."

He said that he had filed an appeal, which cited logical and factual inconsistencies in the trial. For instance, one medical examiner said that Janiszewski had drowned, whereas another insisted that he had died of strangulation. The judge herself had admitted that she was not sure if Bala had carried out the crime alone or with an accomplice.

When I asked him about "Amok," Bala became animated and gave direct and detailed answers. "The thesis of the book is not my personal thesis," he said. "I'm not an anti-feminist. I'm not a chauvinist. I'm not heartless. Chris, in many places, is my anti-hero." Several times, he pointed to my pad and said, "Put this down" or "This is important." As he watched me taking notes, he said, with a hint of awe, "You see how crazy this is? You are here writing a story about a story I made up about a murder that never happened." On virtually every page of his copy of "Amok," he had underlined passages and scribbled notations in the margins. Later, he showed me several scraps of paper on which he had drawn elaborate diagrams revealing his literary influences. It was clear that, in prison, he had become even more consumed by the book. "I sometimes read pages aloud to my cellmates," he said.

One question that was never answered at the trial still

hovered over the case: Why would someone commit a murder and then write about it in a novel that would help to get him caught? In "Crime and Punishment," Raskolnikov speculates that even the smartest criminal makes mistakes, because he "experiences at the moment of the crime a sort of failure of will and reason, which . . . are replaced by a phenomenal, childish thoughtlessness, just at the moment when reason and prudence are most necessary." "Amok," however, had been published three years after the murder. If Bala was guilty of murder, the cause was not a "failure of will and reason" but, rather, an excess of both.

Some observers wondered if Bala had wanted to get caught, or, at least, to unburden himself. In "Amok," Chris speaks of having a "guilty conscience" and of his desire to remove his "white gloves of silence." Though Bala maintained his innocence, it was possible to read the novel as a kind of confession. Wroblewski and the authorities, who believed that Bala's greatest desire was to attain literary immortality, saw his crime and his writing as indivisible. At the trial, Janiszewski's widow pleaded with the press to stop making Bala out to be an artist rather than a murderer. Since his arrest, "Amok" had become a sensation in Poland, selling out at virtually every bookstore.

"There's going to be a new edition coming out with an afterword about the trial and all the events that have happened," Bala told me excitedly. "Other countries are interested in publishing it as well." Flipping through the pages of his own copy, he added, "There's never been a book quite like this."

As we spoke, he seemed far less interested in the idea of the "perfect crime" than he was in the "perfect story," which, in his definition, pushed past the boundaries of aesthetics and reality and morality charted by his literary forebears. "You know, I'm working on a sequel to 'Amok,'" he said, his eyes lighting up. "It's called 'De Liryk.'" He repeated the words several times. "It's a pun. It means 'lyrics,' as in a story, or 'delirium.'"

He explained that he had started the new book before he was arrested, but that the police had seized his computer, which contained his only copy. (He was trying to get the files back.) The authorities told me that they had found in the computer evidence that Bala was collecting information on Stasia's new boyfriend, Harry. "Single, 34 years old, his mom died when he was 8," Bala had written. "Apparently works at the railway company, probably as a train driver but I'm not sure." Wroblewski and the authorities suspected that Harry might be Bala's next target. After Bala had learned that Harry visited an Internet chat room, he had posted a message at the site, under an assumed name, saying, "Sorry to bother you but I'm looking for Harry. Does anyone know him from Chojnow?"

Bala told me that he hoped to complete his second novel after the appeals court made its ruling. In fact, several weeks after we spoke, the court, to the disbelief of many, annulled the original verdict. Although the appeals panel found an "undoubted connection" between Bala and the murder, it concluded that there were still gaps in the "logical chain of evidence," such as the medical examiners' conflicting testimony, which needed to be resolved. The panel refused to release Bala from prison, but ordered a new trial.

Bala insisted that, no matter what happened, he would finish "De Liryk." He glanced at the guards, as if afraid they might hear him, then leaned forward and whispered, "This book is going to be even more shocking."

—*February, 2008*

In December of 2008, Bala received a new trial. Once more, he was found guilty. He is currently serving a twenty-five-year sentence.

The Chameleon

On May 3, 2005, in France, a man called an emergency hot line for missing and exploited children. He frantically explained that he was a tourist passing through Orthez, near the western Pyrenees, and that at the train station he had encountered a fifteen-year-old boy who was alone, and terrified. Another hot line received a similar call, and the boy eventually arrived, by himself, at a local government child-welfare office. Slender and short, with pale skin and trembling hands, he wore a muffler around much of his face and had a baseball cap pulled over his eyes. He had no money and carried little more than a cell phone and an I.D., which said that his name was Francisco Hernandez Fernandez and that he was born on December 13, 1989, in Cáceres, Spain. Initially, he barely spoke, but after some prodding he revealed that his parents and younger brother had been killed in a car accident. The crash left him in a coma for several weeks and, upon recovering, he was sent to live with an uncle, who abused him. Finally, he fled to France, where his mother had grown up.

French authorities placed Francisco at the St. Vincent de Paul shelter in the nearby city of Pau. A state-run institution that housed about thirty-five boys and girls, most of whom had been either removed from dysfunctional families or abandoned, the shelter was in an old stone building with peeling white wooden shutters; on the roof was a statue of St. Vincent protecting a child in the folds of his gown. Francisco was given a single room, and he seemed relieved to be able to wash and change in private: his head and body, he explained, were covered in burns and scars from the car accident. He was enrolled at the Collège Jean Monnet, a local secondary school that had four hundred or so students, mostly from tough neighborhoods, and that had a reputation for violence. Although students were forbidden to wear hats, the principal at the time, Claire Chadourne, made an exception for Francisco, who said that he feared being teased about his scars. Like many of the social workers and teachers who dealt with Francisco, Chadourne, who had been an educator for more than thirty years, felt protective toward him. With his baggy pants and his cell phone dangling from a cord around his neck, he looked

like a typical teen-ager, but he seemed deeply trauma-
tized. He never changed his clothes in front of the other
students in gym class, and resisted being subjected to a
medical exam. He spoke softly, with his head bowed,
and recoiled if anyone tried to touch him.

Gradually, Francisco began hanging out with other
kids at recess and participating in class. Since he had
enrolled so late in the school year, his literature teacher
asked another student, Rafael Pessoa De Almeida, to
help him with his coursework. Before long, Francisco
was helping Rafael. "This guy can learn like lightning,"
Rafael recalls thinking.

One day after school, Rafael asked Francisco if he
wanted to go ice-skating, and the two became friends,
playing video games and sharing school gossip. Rafael
sometimes picked on his younger brother, and Francisco,
recalling that he used to mistreat his own sibling, advised,
"Make sure you love your brother and stay close."

At one point, Rafael borrowed Francisco's cell phone;
to his surprise, its address book and call log were pro-
tected by security codes. When Rafael returned the
phone, Francisco displayed a photograph on its screen of
a young boy who looked just like Francisco. "That's my
brother," he said.

Francisco was soon one of the most popular kids in
school, dazzling classmates with his knowledge of music
and arcane slang—he even knew American idioms—and

moving effortlessly between rival cliques. "The students loved him," a teacher recalls. "He had this aura about him, this charisma."

During tryouts for a talent show, the music teacher asked Francisco if he was interested in performing. He handed her a CD to play, then walked to the end of the room and tilted his hat flamboyantly, waiting for the music to start. As Michael Jackson's song "Unbreakable" filled the room, Francisco started to dance like the pop star, twisting his limbs and lip-synching the words "You can't believe it, you can't conceive it / And you can't touch me, 'cause I'm untouchable." Everyone in the room watched in awe. "He didn't just look like Michael Jackson," the music teacher subsequently recalled. "He *was* Michael Jackson."

Later, in computer class, Francisco showed Rafael an Internet image of a small reptile with a slithery tongue.

"What is it?" Rafael asked.

"A chameleon," Francisco replied.

On June 8th, an administrator rushed into the principal's office. She said that she had been watching a television program the other night about one of the world's most infamous impostors: Frédéric Bourdin, a thirty-year-old Frenchman who serially impersonated children. "I swear to God, Bourdin looks exactly like Francisco Hernandez Fernandez," the administrator said.

Chadourne was incredulous: thirty would make Fran-

cisco older than some of her teachers. She did a quick
Internet search for "Frédéric Bourdin." Hundreds of
news items came up about the "king of impostors" and the
"master of new identities," who, like Peter Pan, "didn't
want to grow up." A photograph of Bourdin closely
resembled Francisco—there was the same formidable
chin, the same gap between the front teeth. Chadourne
called the police.

"Are you sure it's him?" an officer asked.

"No, but I have this strange feeling."

When the police arrived, Chadourne sent the assistant
principal to summon Francisco from class. As Francisco
entered Chadourne's office, the police seized him and
thrust him against the wall, causing her to panic: what if
he really was an abused orphan? Then, while handcuff-
ing Bourdin, the police removed his baseball cap. There
were no scars on his head; rather, he was going bald. "I
want a lawyer," he said, his voice suddenly dropping to
that of a man.

At police headquarters, he admitted that he was Frédéric Bourdin, and that in the past decade and a half
he had invented scores of identities, in more than fifteen countries and five languages. His aliases included
Benjamin Kent, Jimmy Morins, Alex Dole, Sladjan Ras-
kovic, Arnaud Orions, Giovanni Petrullo, and Michelangelo Martini. News reports claimed that he had even
impersonated a tiger tamer and a priest, but, in truth, he

had nearly always played a similar character: an abused
or abandoned child. He was unusually adept at trans-
forming his appearance—his facial hair, his weight, his
walk, his mannerisms. "I can become whatever I want,"
he liked to say. In 2004, when he pretended to be a
fourteen-year-old French boy in the town of Grenoble,
a doctor who examined him at the request of authorities concluded that he was, indeed, a teen-ager. A police
captain in Pau noted, "When he talked in Spanish, he
became a Spaniard. When he talked in English, he was
an Englishman." Chadourne said of him, "Of course, he
lied, but what an actor!"

Over the years, Bourdin had insinuated himself into
youth shelters, orphanages, foster homes, junior high
schools, and children's hospitals. His trail of cons extended
to, among other places, Spain, Germany, Belgium, England, Ireland, Italy, Luxembourg, Switzerland, Bosnia,
Portugal, Austria, Slovakia, France, Sweden, Denmark,
and America. The U.S. State Department warned that
he was an "exceedingly clever" man who posed as a desperate child in order to "win sympathy," and a French
prosecutor called him "an incredible illusionist whose
perversity is matched only by his intelligence." Bourdin
himself has said, "I am a manipulator. . . . My job is to
manipulate."

In Pau, the authorities launched an investigation to
determine why a thirty-year-old man would pose as a

teen-age orphan. They found no evidence of sexual devi-
ance or pedophilia; they did not uncover any financial
motive, either. "In my twenty-two years on the job, I've
never seen a case like it," Eric Maurel, the prosecutor,
told me. "Usually people con for money. His profit seems
to have been purely emotional."

On his right forearm, police discovered a tattoo. It
said *"caméléon nantais"*—"Chameleon from Nantes."

"Mr. Grann," Bourdin said, politely extending his
hand to me. We were on a street in the center of Pau,
where he had agreed to meet me one morning in the
fall of 2007. For once, he seemed unmistakably an adult,
with a faint five-o'clock shadow. He was dressed theat-
rically, in white pants, a white shirt, a checkered vest,
white shoes, a blue satin bow tie, and a foppish hat. Only
the gap between his teeth evoked the memory of Francisco Hernandez Fernandez.

After his ruse in Pau had been exposed, Bourdin
moved to a village in the Pyrenees, twenty-five miles
away. "I wanted to escape from all the glare," he said.
As had often been the case with Bourdin's deceptions,
the authorities were not sure how to punish him. Psy-
chiatrists determined that he was sane. ("Is he a psychopath?" one doctor testified. "Absolutely not.") No statute
seemed to fit his crime. Ultimately, he was charged with

obtaining and using a fake I.D., and received a six-month suspended sentence.

A local reporter, Xavier Sota, told me that since then Bourdin had periodically appeared in Pau, always in a different guise. Sometimes he had a mustache or a beard. Sometimes his hair was tightly cropped; at other times, it was straggly. Sometimes he dressed like a rapper, and on other occasions like a businessman. "It was as if he were trying to find a new character to inhabit," Sota said.

Bourdin and I sat down on a bench near the train station, as a light rain began to fall. A car paused by the curb in front of us, with a couple inside. They rolled down the window, peered out, and said to each other, "*Le Caméléon.*"

"I am quite famous in France these days," Bourdin said. "Too famous."

As we spoke, his large brown eyes flitted across me, seemingly taking me in. One of his police interrogators called him a "human recorder." To my surprise, Bourdin knew where I had worked, where I was born, the name of my wife, even what my sister and brother did for a living. "I like to know whom I'm meeting," he said.

Aware of how easy it is to deceive others, he was paranoid of being a mark. "I don't trust anybody," he said. For a person who described himself as a "professional liar," he seemed oddly fastidious about the facts of his own life. "I don't want you to make me into somebody

I'm not," he said. "The story is good enough without embellishment."

I knew that Bourdin had grown up in and around Nantes, and I asked him about his tattoo. Why would someone who tried to erase his identity leave a trace of one? He rubbed his arm where the words were imprinted on his skin. Then he said, "I will tell you the truth behind all my lies."

Before he was Benjamin Kent or Michelangelo Martini—before he was the child of an English judge or an Italian diplomat—he was Frédéric Pierre Bourdin, the illegitimate son of Ghislaine Bourdin, who was eighteen and poor when she gave birth to him, in a suburb of Paris, on June 13, 1974. On government forms, Frédéric's father is often listed as "X," meaning that his identity was unknown. But Ghislaine, during an interview at her small house in a rural area in western France, told me that "X" was a twenty-five-year-old Algerian immigrant named Kaci, whom she had met at a margarine factory where they both worked. (She says that she can no longer remember his last name.) After she became pregnant, she discovered that Kaci was already married, and so she left her job and did not tell him that she was carrying his child.

Ghislaine raised Frédéric until he was two and

a half—"He was like any other child, totally normal," she says—at which time child services intervened at the behest of her parents. A relative says of Ghislaine, "She liked to drink and dance and stay out at night. She didn't want anything to do with that child." Ghislaine insists that she had obtained another factory job and was perfectly competent, but the judge placed Frédéric in her parents' custody. Years later, Ghislaine wrote Frédéric a letter, telling him, "You are my son and they stole you from me at the age of two. They did everything to separate us from each other and we have become two strangers."

Frédéric says that his mother had a dire need for attention and, on the rare occasions that he saw her, she would feign being deathly ill and make him run to get help. "To see me frightened gave her pleasure," he says. Though Ghislaine denies this, she acknowledges that she once attempted suicide and her son had to rush to find assistance.

When Frédéric was five, he moved with his grandparents to Mouchamps, a hamlet southeast of Nantes. Frédéric—part Algerian and fatherless, and dressed in secondhand clothes from Catholic charities—was a village outcast, and in school he began to tell fabulous stories about himself. He said that his father was never around because he was a "British secret agent." One of his elementary-school teachers, Yvon Bourgueil, describes

Bourdin as a precocious and captivating child, who had
an extraordinary imagination and visual sense, drawing
wild, beautiful comic strips. "He had this way of making
you connect to him," Bourgueil recalls. He also noticed
signs of mental distress. At one point, Frédéric told his
grandparents that he had been molested by a neighbor,
though nobody in the tightly knit village investigated the
allegation. In one of his comic strips, Frédéric depicted
himself drowning in a river. He increasingly misbehaved,
acting out in class and stealing from neighbors. At twelve,
he was sent to live at Les Grézillières, a private facility
for juveniles, in Nantes.

There, his "little dramas," as one of his teachers called
them, became more fanciful. Bourdin often pretended to
be an amnesiac, intentionally getting lost in the streets.
In 1990, after he turned sixteen, Frédéric was forced to
move to another youth home, and he soon ran away.
He hitchhiked to Paris, where, scared and hungry, he
invented his first fake character: he approached a police
officer and told him that he was a lost British teen named
Jimmy Sale. "I dreamed they would send me to England,
where I always imagined life was more beautiful," he
recalls. When the police discovered that he spoke almost
no English, he admitted his deceit and was returned to
the youth home. But he had devised what he calls his
"technique," and in this fashion he began to wander
across Europe, moving in and out of orphanages and fos-

ter homes, searching for the "perfect shelter." In 1991, he was found in a train station in Langres, France, pretending to be sick, and was placed in a children's hospital in Saint-Dizier. According to his medical report, no one knew "who he was or where he came from." Answering questions only in writing, he indicated that his name was Frédéric Cassis—a play on his real father's first name, Kaci. Frédéric's doctor, Jean-Paul Milanese, wrote in a letter to a child-welfare judge, "We find ourselves confronted with a young runaway teen, mute, having broken with his former life."

On a piece of paper, Bourdin scribbled what he wanted most: "A home and a school. That's all."

When doctors started to unravel his past, a few months later, Bourdin confessed his real identity and moved on. "I would rather leave on my own than be taken away," he told me. During his career as an impostor, Bourdin often voluntarily disclosed the truth, as if the attention that came from exposure were as thrilling as the con itself.

On June 13, 1992, after he had posed as more than a dozen fictional children, Bourdin turned eighteen, becoming a legal adult. "I'd been in shelters and foster homes most of my life, and suddenly I was told, 'That's it. You're free to go,'" he recalls. "How could I become something I could not imagine?" In November, 1993, posing as a mute child, he lay down in the middle of a street in the French town of Auch and was taken by firemen to a hospital. *La Dépêche du Midi*, a local news-paper, ran a story about him, asking, "Where does this mute adolescent . . . come from?" The next day, the paper published another article, under the headline "THE MUTE ADOLESCENT WHO APPEARED OUT OF NOWHERE HAS STILL NOT REVEALED HIS SECRET." After fleeing, he was caught attempting a similar ruse nearby and admitted that he was Frédéric Bourdin. "THE MUTE OF AUCH SPEAKS FOUR LANGUAGES," *La Dépêche du Midi* proclaimed.

As Bourdin assumed more and more identities, he attempted to kill off his real one. One day, the mayor of Mouchamps received a call from the "German police" notifying him that Bourdin's body had been found in Munich. When Bourdin's mother was told the news, she recalls, "My heart stopped." Members of Bourdin's family waited for a coffin to arrive, but it never did. "It was Frédéric playing one of his cruel games," his mother says.

By the mid-nineties, Bourdin had accumulated a criminal record for lying to police and magistrates, and Interpol and other authorities were increasingly on the lookout for him. His activities were also garnering media attention. In 1995, the producers of a popular French television show called "Everything Is Possible" invited him on the program. As Bourdin appeared onstage, looking pale and prepubescent, the host teasingly asked the audience, "What's this boy's name? Michael, Jürgen,

Kevin, or Pedro? What's his real age—thirteen, fourteen, fifteen?" Pressed about his motivations, Bourdin again insisted that all he wanted was love and a family. It was the same rationale he always gave, and, as a result, he was the rare impostor who elicited sympathy as well as anger from those he had duped. (His mother has a less charitable interpretation of her son's stated motive: "He wants to justify what he has become.")

The producers of "Everything Is Possible" were so affected by his story that they offered him a job in the station's newsroom, but he soon ran off to create more "interior fictions," as one of the producers later told a reporter. At times, Bourdin's deceptions were viewed in existential terms. One of his devotees in France created a Web site that celebrated his shape-shifting, hailing him as an "actor of life and an apostle of a new philosophy of human identity."

One day when I was visiting Bourdin, he described how he transformed himself into a child. Like the impostors he had seen in films such as "Catch Me If You Can," he tried to elevate his criminality into an "art." First, he said, he conceived of a child whom he wanted to play. Then he gradually mapped out the character's biography, from his heritage to his family to his tics. "The key is actually not lying about everything," Bourdin said.

"Otherwise, you'll just mix things up." He said that he adhered to maxims such as "Keep it simple" and "A good liar uses the truth." In choosing a name, he preferred one that carried a deep association in his memory, like Cassis. "The one thing you better not forget is your name," he said.

He compared what he did to being a spy: you changed superficial details while keeping your core intact. This approach not only made it easier to convince people; it allowed him to protect a part of his self, to hold on to some moral center. "I know I can be cruel, but I don't want to become a monster," he said.

Once he had imagined a character, he fashioned a commensurate appearance—meticulously shaving his face, plucking his eyebrows, using hair-removal creams. He often put on baggy pants and a shirt with long sleeves that swallowed his wrists, emphasizing his smallness. Peering in a mirror, he asked himself if others would see what he wanted them to see. "The worst thing you can do is deceive yourself," he said.

When he honed an identity, it was crucial to find some element of the character that he shared—a technique employed by many actors. "People always say to me, 'Why don't you become an actor?'" he told me. "I think I would be a very good actor, like Arnold Schwarzenegger or Sylvester Stallone. But I don't want to play somebody. I want to *be* somebody."

In order to help ease his character into the real world, he fostered the illusion among local authorities that his character actually existed. As he had done in Orthez, he would call a hot line and claim to have seen the character in a perilous situation. The authorities were less likely to grill a child who appeared to be in distress. If someone noticed that Bourdin looked oddly mature, however, he did not object. "A teen-ager wants to look older," he said. "I treat it like a compliment."

Though he emphasized his cunning, he acknowledged what any con man knows but rarely admits: it is not that hard to fool people. People have basic expectations of others' behavior and are rarely on guard for someone to subvert them. By playing on some primal need—vanity, greed, loneliness—men like Bourdin make their mark further suspend disbelief. As a result, most cons are filled with logical inconsistencies, even absurdities, which seem humiliatingly obvious after the fact. Bourdin, who generally tapped into a mark's sense of goodness rather than into some darker urge, says, "Nobody expects a seemingly vulnerable child to be lying."

In October, 1997, Bourdin told me, he was at a youth home in Linares, Spain. A child-welfare judge who was handling his case had given him twenty-four hours to prove that he was a teen-ager; otherwise, she would take his fingerprints, which were on file with Interpol. Bourdin knew that, as an adult with a criminal record, he would likely face prison. He had already tried to run away once and was caught, and the staff was keeping an eye on his whereabouts. And so he did something that both stretched the bounds of credulity and threatened to transform him into the kind of "monster" that he had insisted he never wanted to become. Rather than invent an identity, he stole one. He assumed the persona of a missing sixteen-year-old boy from Texas. Bourdin, now twenty-three, not only had to convince the authorities that he was an American child; he had to convince the missing boy's family.

According to Bourdin, the plan came to him in the middle of the night: if he could fool the judge into thinking that he was an American, he might be let go. He asked permission to use the telephone in the shelter's office and called the National Center for Missing and Exploited Children, in Alexandria, Virginia, trolling for a real identity. Speaking in English, which he had picked up during his travels, he claimed that his name was Jonathan Durean and that he was a director of the Linares shelter. He said that a frightened child had turned up who would not disclose his identity but who spoke English with an American accent. Bourdin offered a description of the boy that matched himself—short, slight, prominent chin, brown hair, a gap between his teeth—and asked if the center had anyone similar in its database. After searching, Bourdin recalls, a woman at the center said that the boy might be Nicholas Barclay, who had been reported missing in San Antonio on June 13, 1994, at the age of thirteen. Barclay was last seen, according to his file, wearing "a white T-shirt, purple pants, black tennis shoes and carrying a pink backpack."

Adopting a skeptical tone, Bourdin says, he asked if the center could send any more information that it had regarding Barclay. The woman said that she would mail overnight Barclay's missing-person flyer and immediately fax a copy as well. After giving her the fax number in the office he was borrowing, Bourdin says, he hung up and waited. Peeking out the door, he looked to see if anyone was coming. The hallway was dark and quiet, but he could hear footsteps. At last, a copy of the flyer emerged from the fax machine. The printout was so faint that most of it was illegible. Still, the photograph's resemblance to him did not seem that far off. "I can do this," Bourdin recalls thinking. He quickly called back the center, he says, and told the woman, "I have some good news. Nicholas Barclay is standing right beside me."

Elated, she gave him the number of the officer in the San Antonio Police Department who was in charge of the investigation. This time pretending to be a Spanish policeman, Bourdin says, he phoned the officer and, mentioning details about Nicholas that he had learned

from the woman at the center—such as the pink backpack—declared that the missing child had been found.
The officer said that he would contact the F.B.I. and the
U.S. Embassy in Madrid. Bourdin had not fully contemplated what he was about to unleash.

The next day at the Linares shelter, Bourdin inter-
cepted a package from the National Center for Missing
and Exploited Children addressed to Jonathan Durean.
He ripped open the envelope. Inside was a clean copy
of Nicholas Barclay's missing-person flyer. It showed a
color photograph of a small, fair-skinned boy with blue
eyes and brown hair so light that it appeared almost
blond. The flyer listed several identifying features, including a cross tattooed between Barclay's right index
finger and thumb. Bourdin stared at the picture and said
to himself, "I'm dead." Not only did Bourdin not have
the same tattoo; his eyes and hair were dark brown. In
haste, he burned the flyer in the shelter's courtyard, then
went into the bathroom and bleached his hair. Finally,
he had a friend, using a needle and ink from a pen, give
him a makeshift tattoo resembling Barclay's.

Still, there was the matter of Bourdin's eyes. He tried
to conceive of a story that would explain his appearance.
What if he had been abducted by a child sex ring and
flown to Europe, where he had been tortured and abused,
even experimented on? Yes, that could explain the eyes.
His kidnappers had injected his pupils with chemicals.

He had lost his Texas accent because, for more than three years of captivity, he had been forbidden to speak English. He had escaped from a locked room in a house in Spain when a guard carelessly left the door open. It was a crazy tale, one that violated his maxim to "keep it simple," but it would have to do.

Soon after, the phone in the office rang. Bourdin took the call. It was Nicholas Barclay's thirty-one-year-old half sister, Carey Gibson. "My God, Nicky, is that you?" she asked.

Bourdin didn't know how to respond. He adopted a muffled voice, then said, "Yes, it's me."

Nicholas's mother, Beverly, got on the phone. A tough, heavyset woman with a broad face and dyed-brown hair, she worked the graveyard shift at a Dunkin' Donuts in San Antonio seven nights a week. She had never married Nicholas's father and had raised Nicholas with her two older children, Carey and Jason. (She was divorced from Carey and Jason's father, though she still used her married name, Dollarhide.) A heroin addict, she had struggled during Nicholas's youth to get off drugs. After he disappeared, she had begun to use heroin again and was now addicted to methadone. Despite these difficulties, Carey says, Beverly was not a bad mother: "She was maybe the most functioning drug addict. We had nice things, a nice place, never went without food." Perhaps compensating for the instability in her life, Beverly

fanatically followed a routine: working at the doughnut shop from 10 P.M. to 5 A.M., then stopping at the
Make My Day Lounge to shoot pool and have a few
beers, before going home to sleep. She had a hardness
about her, with a cigarette-roughened voice, but people
who know her also spoke to me of her kindness. After
her night shift, she delivered any leftover doughnuts to a
homeless shelter.

Beverly pulled the phone close to her ear. After the
childlike voice on the other end said that he wanted
to come home, she told me, "I was dumbfounded and
blown away."

Carey, who was married and had two children of her
own, had often held the family together during Beverly's
struggles with drug addiction. Since Nicholas's disappearance, her mother and brother had never seemed
the same, and all Carey wanted was to make the family whole again. She volunteered to go to Spain to bring
Nicholas home, and the packing-and-shipping company
where she worked in sales support offered to pay her fare.

When she arrived at the shelter, a few days later,
accompanied by an official from the U.S. Embassy,
Bourdin had secluded himself in a room. What he had
done, he concedes, was evil. But if he had any moral res-
ervations they did not stop him, and after wrapping his
face in a scarf and putting on a hat and sunglasses he
came out of the room. He was sure that Carey would

instantly realize that he wasn't her brother. Instead, she rushed toward him and hugged him.

Carey was, in many ways, an ideal mark. "My daughter has the best heart and is so easy to manipulate," Beverly says. Carey had never travelled outside the United States, except for partying in Tijuana, and was unfamiliar with European accents and with Spain. After Nicholas disappeared, she had often watched television news programs about lurid child abductions. In addition to feeling the pressure of having received money from her company to make the trip, she had the burden of deciding, as her family's representative, whether this was her long-lost brother.

Though Bourdin referred to her as "Carey" rather than "sis," as Nicholas always had, and though he had a trace of a French accent, Carey says that she had little doubt that it was Nicholas. Not when he could attribute any inconsistencies to his unspeakable ordeal. Not when his nose now looked so much like her uncle Pat's. Not when he had the same tattoo as Nicholas and seemed to know so many details about her family, asking about relatives by name. "Your heart takes over and you want to believe," Carey says.

She showed Bourdin photographs of the family and he studied each one: this is my mother; this is my half brother; this is my grandfather.

Neither American nor Spanish officials raised any

questions once Carey had vouched for him. Nicholas
had been gone for only three years, and the F.B.I. was
not primed to be suspicious of someone claiming to be
a missing child. (The agency told me that, to its knowledge, it had never worked on a case like Bourdin's before.)
According to authorities in Madrid, Carey swore under
oath that Bourdin was her brother and an American citi-
zen. He was granted a U.S. passport and, the next day,
he was on a flight to San Antonio.

For a moment, Bourdin fantasized that he was about
to become part of a real family, but halfway to America
he began to "freak out," as Carey puts it, trembling and
sweating. As she tried to comfort him, he told her that
he thought the plane was going to crash, which, he later
said, is what he wanted: how else could he escape from
what he had done?

When the plane landed, on October 18, 1997,
members of Nicholas's family were waiting for him at
the airport. Bourdin recognized them from Carey's
photographs: Beverly, Nicholas's mother; Carey's then
husband, Bryan Gibson; Bryan and Carey's fourteen-
year-old son, Codey, and their ten-year-old daughter,
Chantel. Only Nicholas's brother, Jason, who was a
recovering drug addict and living in San Antonio, was
absent. A friend of the family videotaped the reunion,
and Bourdin can be seen bundled up, his hat pulled
down, his brown eyes shielded by sunglasses, his already

fading tattoo covered by gloves. Though Bourdin had thought that Nicholas's relatives were going to "hang" him, they rushed to embrace him, saying how much they had missed him. "We were all just emotionally crazy," Codey recalls. Nicholas's mother, however, hung back. "She just didn't seem excited" the way you'd expect from someone "seeing her son," Chantel told me.

Bourdin wondered if Beverly doubted that he was Nicholas, but eventually she, too, greeted him. They all got in Carey's Lincoln Town Car and stopped at McDonald's for cheeseburgers and fries. As Carey recalls it, "He was just sitting by my mom, talking to my son," saying how much "he missed school and asking when he'd see Jason."

Bourdin went to stay with Carey and Bryan rather than live with Beverly. "I work nights and didn't think it was good to leave him alone," Beverly said. Carey and Bryan owned a trailer home in a desolate wooded area in Spring Branch, thirty-five miles north of San Antonio, and Bourdin stared out the window as the car wound along a dirt road, past rusted trucks on cinder blocks and dogs barking at the sound of the engine. As Codey puts it, "We didn't have no Internet, or stuff like that. You can walk all the way to San Antonio before you get any kind of communication."

Their cramped trailer home was not exactly the vision of America that Bourdin had imagined from movies. He shared a room with Codey, and slept on a foam mattress on the floor. Bourdin knew that, if he were to become Nicholas and to continue to fool even his family, he had to learn everything about him, and he began to mine information, secretly rummaging through drawers and picture albums, and watching home videos. When Bourdin discovered a detail about Nicholas's past from one family member, he would repeat it to another. He pointed out, for example, that Bryan once got mad at Nicholas for knocking Codey out of a tree. "He knew that story," Codey recalls, still amazed by the amount of intelligence that Bourdin acquired about the family. Beverly noticed that Bourdin knelt in front of the television, just as Nicholas had. Various members of the family told me that when Bourdin seemed more standoffish than Nicholas or spoke with a strange accent they assumed that it was because of the terrible treatment that he said he had suffered.

As Bourdin came to inhabit the life of Nicholas, he was struck by what he considered to be uncanny similarities between them. Nicholas had been reported missing on Bourdin's birthday. Both came from poor, broken families; Nicholas had almost no relationship with his father, who for a long time didn't know that Nicholas was his son. Nicholas was a sweet, lonely, combustible kid who craved attention and was often in trouble at school. He had been caught stealing a pair of tennis shoes, and his mother had planned to put him in a youth home. ("I couldn't handle him," Beverly recalls. "I couldn't control him.") When Nicholas was young, he was a diehard Michael Jackson fan who had collected all the singer's records and even owned a red leather jacket like the one Jackson wears in his "Thriller" video.

According to Beverly, Bourdin quickly "blended in." He was enrolled in high school and did his homework each night, chastising Codey when he failed to study. He played Nintendo with Codey and watched movies with the family on satellite TV. When he saw Beverly, he hugged her and said, "Hi, Mom." Occasionally on Sundays, he attended church with other members of the family. "He was really nice," Chantel recalls. "Really friendly." Once, when Carey was shooting a home movie of Bourdin, she asked him what he was thinking. "It's really good to have my family and be home again," he replied.

On November 1st, not long after Bourdin had settled into his new home, Charlie Parker, a private investigator, was sitting in his office in San Antonio. The room was crammed with hidden cameras that he deployed in the field: one was attached to a pair of eyeglasses, another was lodged inside a fountain pen, and a third was concealed on the handlebars of a ten-speed bicycle. On a wall hung a photograph that Parker had taken during a stakeout: it showed a married woman with her lover, peeking out of an apartment window. Parker, who had been hired by the woman's husband, called it the "money shot."

Parker's phone rang. It was a television producer from the tabloid show "Hard Copy," who had heard about the extraordinary return of sixteen-year-old Nicholas Barclay and wanted to hire Parker to help investigate the kidnapping. He agreed to take the job.

With silver hair and a raspy voice, Parker, who was then in his late fifties, appeared to have stepped out of a dime novel. When he bought himself a bright-red Toyota convertible, he said to friends, "How ya like that for an old man?" Though Parker had always dreamed about being a P.I., he had only recently become one, having spent thirty years selling lumber and building materials. In 1994, Parker met a San Antonio couple whose twenty-nine-year-old daughter had been raped and fatally stabbed. The case was unsolved, and he began investigating the crime each night after coming home from work. When he discovered that a recently paroled murderer had lived next door to the victim, Parker staked out the man's house, peering out from a white van through infrared goggles. The suspect was soon arrested and ultimately convicted of the murder. Captivated by the experience, Parker formed a "murders club," dedicated to solving cold cases. (Its members included a college psychology professor, a lawyer, and a fry cook.) Within months, the club had uncovered evidence that helped to convict a member of the Air Force who had strangled a fourteen-year-old girl. In 1995, Parker received his license as a private investigator, and he left his life in the lumber business behind.

After Parker spoke with the "Hard Copy" producer, he easily traced Nicholas Barclay to Carey and Bryan's trailer. On November 6th, Parker arrived there with a producer and a camera crew. The family didn't want Bourdin to speak to reporters. "I'm a very private person," Carey says. But Bourdin, who had been in the country for nearly three weeks, agreed to talk. "I wanted the attention at the time," he says. "It was a psychological need. Today, I wouldn't do it."

Parker stood off to one side, listening intently as the young man relayed his harrowing story. "He was calm as a cucumber," Parker told me. "No looking down, no body language. None." But Parker was puzzled by his curious accent.

Parker spied a photograph on a shelf of Nicholas Barclay as a young boy, and kept looking at it and at the person in front of him, thinking that something was amiss. Having once read that ears are distinct, like fingerprints, he went up to the cameraman and whispered, "Zoom in on his ears. Get 'em as close as you can."

Parker slipped the photograph of Nicholas Barclay into his pocket, and after the interview he hurried back to his office and used a scanner to transfer the photo to his computer; he then studied video from the "Hard Copy" interview. Parker zeroed in on the ears in both pictures. "The ears were close, but they didn't match," he says.

Parker called several ophthalmologists and asked if eyes could be changed from blue to brown by injecting chemicals. The doctors said no. Parker also phoned a dialect expert at Trinity University, in San Antonio, who told him that, even if someone had been held in captivity for three years, he would quickly regain his native accent.

Parker passed his suspicions on to the authorities, even though the San Antonio police had declared that "the boy who came back claiming to be Nicholas Barclay is Nicholas Barclay." Fearing that a dangerous stranger was living with Nicholas's family, Parker phoned Beverly and told her what he had discovered. As he recalls the conversation, he said, "It's not him, ma'am. It's not him."

"What do you mean, it's not him?" she asked.

Parker explained about the ears and the eyes and the accent. In his files, Parker wrote, "Family is upset but maintains that they believe it is their son."

Parker says that a few days later he received an angry call from Bourdin. Although Bourdin denies that he made the call, Parker noted in his file at the time that Bourdin said, "Who do you think you are?" When

Parker replied that he didn't believe he was Nicholas, Bourdin shot back, "Immigration thinks it's me. The family thinks it's me."

Parker wondered if he should let the matter go. He had tipped off the authorities and was no longer under contract to investigate the matter. He had other cases piling up. And he figured that a mother would know her own son. Still, the boy's accent sounded French, maybe French Moroccan. If so, what was a foreigner doing infiltrating a trailer home in the backwoods of Texas? "I thought he was a terrorist, I swear to God," Parker says.

Beverly rented a small room in a run-down apartment complex in San Antonio, and Parker started to follow Bourdin when he visited her. "I'd set up on the apartment, and watch him come out," Parker says. "He would walk all the way to the bus stop, wearing his Walkman and doing his Michael Jackson moves."

Bourdin was struggling to stay in character. He found living with Carey and Bryan "claustrophobic," and was happiest when he was outside, wandering the streets. "I was not used to being in someone else's family, to live with them like I'm one of theirs," he says. "I wasn't ready for it." One day, Carey and the family presented him with a cardboard box. Inside were Nicholas's baseball cards, records, and various mementos. He picked up each item, gingerly. There was a letter from one of Nicholas's girlfriends. As he read it, he said to himself, "I'm not this boy."

After two months in the United States, Bourdin started to come apart. He was moody and aloof—"weirding out," as Codey put it. He stopped attending classes (one student tauntingly said that he sounded "like a Norwegian") and was consequently suspended. In December, he took off in Bryan and Carey's car and drove to Oklahoma, with the windows down, listening to Michael Jackson's song "Scream": "Tired of the schemes / The lies are disgusting . . . / Somebody please have mercy / 'Cause I just can't take it." The police pulled him over for speeding, and he was arrested. Beverly, Carey, and Bryan picked him up at the police station and brought him home.

According to his real mother, Ghislaine, Bourdin called her in Europe. For all his disagreements with his mother, Bourdin still seemed to long for her. (He once wrote her a letter, saying, "I don't want to lose you. . . . If you disappear then I disappear.") Ghislaine says Bourdin confided that he was living with a woman in Texas who believed that he was her son. She became so upset that she hung up.

Shortly before Christmas, Bourdin went into the bathroom and looked at himself in the mirror—at his brown eyes, his dyed hair. He grabbed a razor and began to mutilate his face. He was put in the psychiatric ward

of a local hospital for several days of observation. Later,
Bourdin, paraphrasing Nietzsche, wrote in a notebook,
"When you fight monsters, be careful that in the process
you do not become one." He also jotted down a poem:
"My days are phantom days, each one the shadow of a
hope; / My real life never was begun, / Nor any of my
real deeds done."

Doctors judged Bourdin to be stable enough to return
to Carey's trailer. But he remained disquieted, and
increasingly wondered what had happened to the real
Nicholas Barclay. So did Parker, who, while trying to
identify Bourdin, had started to gather information and
interview Nicholas's neighbors. At the time that Nicholas disappeared, he was living with Beverly in a small
one-story house in San Antonio. Nicholas's half brother,
Jason, who was then twenty-four, had recently moved
in with them after living for a period with his cousin, in
Utah. Jason was wiry and strong, with long brown curly
hair and a comb often tucked in the back pocket of his
jeans. He had burn marks on his body and face: at thirteen, he had lit a cigarette after filling a lawn mower with
gasoline and accidentally set himself on fire. Because
of his scars, Carey says, "Jason worried that he would
never meet somebody and he would always be alone." He
strummed Lynyrd Skynyrd songs on his guitar and was a
capable artist who sketched portraits of friends. Though
he had only completed high school, he was bright and

articulate. He also had an addictive personality, like his mother, often drinking heavily and using cocaine. He had his "demons," as Carey put it.

On June 13, 1994, Beverly and Jason told police that Nicholas had been playing basketball three days earlier and called his house from a pay phone, wanting a ride home. Beverly was sleeping, so Jason answered the phone. He told Nicholas to walk home. Nicholas never made it. Because Nicholas had recently fought with his mother over the tennis shoes he had stolen, and over the possibility of being sent to a home for juveniles, the police initially thought that he had run away—even though he hadn't taken any money or possessions.

Parker was surprised by police reports showing that after Nicholas's disappearance there were several disturbances at Beverly's house. On July 12th, she called the police, though when an officer arrived she insisted that she was all right. Jason told the officer that his mother was "drinking and scream[ing] at him because her other son ran away." A few weeks later, Beverly called the police again, about what authorities described as "family violence." The officer on the scene reported that Beverly and Jason were "exchanging words"; Jason was asked to leave the house for the day, and he complied. On September 25th, police received another call, this time from Jason. He claimed that his younger brother had returned and tried to break into the garage, fleeing when Jason spotted him. In his report, the officer on duty said that he had "checked the area" for Nicholas but was "unable to locate him."

Jason's behavior grew even more erratic. He was arrested for "using force" against a police officer, and Beverly kicked him out of the house. Nicholas's disappearance, Codey told me, had "messed Jason up pretty bad. He went on a bad drug binge and was shooting cocaine for a long time." Because he had refused to help Nicholas get a ride home on the day he vanished, Chantel says, Jason had "a lot of guilt."

In late 1996, Jason checked into a rehabilitation center and weaned himself from drugs. After he finished the program, he remained at the facility for more than a year, serving as a counsellor and working for a landscaping business that the center operated. He was still there when Bourdin turned up, claiming to be his missing brother.

Bourdin wondered why Jason had not met him at the airport and had initially made no effort to see him at Carey's. After a month and a half, Bourdin and family members say, Jason finally came for a visit. Even then, Codey says, "Jason was standoffish." Though Jason gave him a hug in front of the others, Bourdin says, he seemed to eye him warily. After a few minutes, Jason told him to come outside, and held out his hand to Bourdin. A necklace with a gold cross glittered in his palm. Jason said that it was for him. "It was like he had to give it to me," Bourdin says. Jason put it around his neck. Then he said goodbye, and never returned.

Bourdin told me, "It was clear that Jason knew what had happened to Nicholas." For the first time, Bourdin began to wonder who was conning whom.

The authorities, meanwhile, had started to doubt Bourdin's story. Nancy Fisher, who at the time was a veteran F.B.I. agent, had interviewed Bourdin several weeks after he arrived in the United States, in order to document his allegations of being kidnapped on American soil. Immediately, she told me, she "smelled a rat": "His hair was dark but bleached blond and the roots were quite obvious."

Parker knew Fisher and had shared with her his own suspicions. Fisher warned Parker not to interfere with a federal probe, but as they conducted parallel investigations they developed a sense of trust, and Parker passed on any information he obtained. When Fisher made inquiries into who may have abducted Nicholas and sexually abused him, she says, she found Beverly oddly "surly and uncooperative."

Fisher wondered whether Beverly and her family simply wanted to believe that Bourdin was their loved one. Whatever the family's motivations, Fisher's main concern was the mysterious figure who had entered the United States. She knew that it was impossible for him to have altered his eye color. In November, under the pretext of getting Bourdin treatment for his alleged abuse, Fisher took him to see a forensic psychiatrist in Houston, who concluded from his syntax and grammar that he could not be American, and was most likely French or Spanish. The F.B.I. shared the results with Beverly and Carey, Fisher says, but they insisted that he was Nicholas.

Believing that Bourdin was a spy, Fisher says, she contacted the Central Intelligence Agency, explaining the potential threat and asking for help in identifying him. "The C.I.A. wouldn't assist me," she says. "I was told by a C.I.A. agent that until you can prove he's European we can't help you. "

Fisher tried to persuade Beverly and Bourdin to give blood samples for a DNA test. Both refused. "Beverly said, 'How dare you say he's not my son,'" Fisher recalls. In the middle of February, four months after Bourdin arrived in the United States, Fisher obtained warrants to force them to cooperate. "I go to her house to get a blood sample, and she lies on the floor and says she's not going to get up," Fisher says. "I said, 'Yes, you are.'"

"Beverly defended me," Bourdin says. "She did her best to stop them."

Along with their blood, Fisher obtained Bourdin's

fingerprints, which she sent to the State Department to see if there was a match with Interpol.

Carey, worried about her supposed brother's self-mutilation and instability, was no longer willing to let him stay with her, and he went to live with Beverly in her apartment. By then, Bourdin claims, he had begun to look at the family differently. His mind retraced a series of curious interactions: Beverly's cool greeting at the airport, Jason's delay in visiting him. He says that, although Carey and Bryan had seemed intent on believing that he was Nicholas—ignoring the obvious evidence—Beverly had treated him less like a son than like a "ghost." One time when he was staying with her, Bourdin alleges, she got drunk and screamed, "I know that God punished me by sending you to me. I don't know who the hell you are. Why the fuck are you doing this?" (Beverly does not remember such an incident but says, "He must have got me pissed off.")

On March 5, 1998, with the authorities closing in on Bourdin, Beverly called Parker and said she believed that Bourdin was an impostor. The next morning, Parker took him to a diner. "I raise my pants so he can see I'm not wearing a gun" in his ankle holster, Parker says. "I want him to relax."

They ordered hotcakes. After nearly five months of pretending to be Nicholas Barclay, Bourdin says, he was psychically frayed. According to Parker, when he told

"Nicholas" that he had upset his "mother," the young man blurted out, "She's not my mother, and you know it."

"You gonna tell me who you are?"

"I'm Frédéric Bourdin and I'm wanted by Interpol."

After a few minutes, Parker went to the men's room and called Nancy Fisher with the news. She had just received the same information from Interpol. "We're trying to get a warrant right now," she told Parker. "Stall him."

Parker went back to the table and continued to talk to Bourdin. As Bourdin spoke about his itinerant life in Europe, Parker says, he felt some guilt for turning him in. Bourdin, who despises Parker and disputes the details of their conversation, accuses the detective of "pretending" to have solved the case; it was as if Parker had intruded into Bourdin's interior fiction and given himself a starring role. After about an hour, Parker drove Bourdin back to Beverly's apartment. As Parker was pulling away, Fisher and the authorities were already descending on him. He surrendered quietly. "I knew I was Frédéric Bourdin again," he says. Beverly reacted less calmly. She turned and yelled at Fisher, "What took you so long?"

In custody, Bourdin told a story that seemed as fanciful as his tale of being Nicholas Barclay. He alleged that Beverly and Jason may have been complicit in Nicholas's disappearance, and that they had known from the outset that Bourdin was lying. "I'm a good impostor, but I'm not that good," Bourdin told me.

Of course, the authorities could not rely on the account of a known pathological liar. "He tells ninety-nine lies and maybe the one hundredth is the truth, but you don't know," Fisher says. Yet the authorities had their own suspicions. Jack Stick, who was a federal prosecutor at the time and who later served a term in the Texas House of Representatives, was assigned Bourdin's case. He and Fisher wondered why Beverly had resisted attempts by the F.B.I. to investigate Bourdin's purported kidnapping and, later, to uncover his deception. They also questioned why she had not taken Bourdin back to live with her. According to Fisher, Carey told her that it was because it was "too upsetting" for Beverly, which, at least to Fisher and Stick, seemed strange. "You'd be so happy to have your child back," Fisher says. It was "another red flag."

Fisher and Stick took note of the disturbances in Beverly's house after Nicholas had vanished, and the police report stating that Beverly was screaming at Jason over Nicholas's disappearance. Then there was Jason's claim that he had witnessed Nicholas breaking into the house. No evidence could be found to back up this startling story, and Jason had made the claim at the time that the police had started "sniffing around," as Stick put it. He and Fisher suspected that the story was a ruse meant to reinforce the idea that Nicholas was a runaway.

Stick and Fisher began to edge toward a homicide investigation. "I wanted to know what had happened to that little kid," Stick recalls.

Stick and Fisher gathered more evidence suggesting that Beverly's home was prone to violence. They say that officials at Nicholas's school had expressed concern that Nicholas might be an abused child, owing to bruises on his body, and that just before he disappeared the officials had alerted child-protective services. And neighbors noted that Nicholas had sometimes hit Beverly.

One day, Fisher asked Beverly to take a polygraph. Carey recalls, "I said, 'Mom, do whatever they ask you to do. Go take the lie-detector test. You didn't kill Nicholas.' So she did."

While Beverly was taking the polygraph, Fisher watched the proceedings on a video monitor in a nearby room. The most important question was whether Beverly currently knew the whereabouts of Nicholas. She said no, twice. The polygraph examiner told Fisher that Beverly had seemingly answered truthfully. When Fisher expressed disbelief, the examiner said that if Beverly was lying, she had to be on drugs. After a while, the examiner administered the test again, at which point the effects of any possible narcotics, including methadone, might have worn off. This time, when the examiner asked if Beverly knew Nicholas's whereabouts, Fisher says, the machine went wild, indicating a lie. "She blew the instruments practically off the table," Fisher says. (False positives are not uncommon in polygraphs, and scientists dispute their basic reliability.)

According to Fisher, when the examiner told Beverly that she had failed the exam, and began pressing her with more questions, Beverly yelled, "I don't have to put up with this," then got up and ran out the door. "I catch her," Fisher recalls. "I say, 'Why are you running?' She is furious. She says, 'This is so typical of Nicholas. Look at the hell he's putting me through.'"

Fisher next wanted to interview Jason, but he resisted. When he finally agreed to meet her, several weeks after Bourdin had been arrested, Fisher says, she had to "pull words out of him." They spoke about the fact that he had not gone to see his alleged brother for nearly two months: "I said, 'Here's your brother, long gone, kidnapped, and aren't you eager to see him?' He said, 'Well, no.' I said, 'Did he look like your brother to you?' 'Well, I guess.'" Fisher found his responses grudging, and developed a "very strong suspicion that Jason had participated in the disappearance of his brother." Stick, too, believed that Jason either had been "involved in Nicholas's disappearance or had information that could tell us what had happened." Fisher even suspected that Beverly knew what had happened to Nicholas, and may have helped cover up the crime in order to protect Jason.

After the interview, Stick and Fisher say, Jason

refused to speak to the authorities again without a lawyer or unless he was under arrest. But Parker, who as a private investigator was not bound by the same legal restrictions as Stick and Fisher, continued to press Jason. On one occasion, he accused him of murder. "I think you did it," Parker says he told him. "I don't think you meant to do it, but you did." In response, Parker says, "He just looked at me."

Several weeks after Fisher and Parker questioned Jason, Parker was driving through downtown San Antonio and saw Beverly on the sidewalk. He asked her if she wanted a ride. When she got in, she told him that Jason had died of an overdose of cocaine. Parker, who knew that Jason had been off drugs for more than a year, says that he asked if she thought he had taken his life on purpose. She said, "I don't know." Stick, Fisher, and Parker suspect that it was a suicide.

Since the loss of her sons, Beverly has stopped using drugs and moved out to Spring Branch, where she lives in a trailer, helping a woman care for her severely handicapped daughter. She agreed to talk with me about the authorities' suspicions. At first, Beverly said that I could drive out to meet her, but later she told me that the woman she worked for did not want visitors, so we spoke by phone. One of her vocal cords had recently become paralyzed, deepening her already low and gravelly voice. Parker, who had frequently chatted with her at the doughnut shop, had told me, "I don't know why I liked her, but I did. She had this thousand-yard stare. She looked like someone whose life had taken everything out of her."

Beverly answered my questions forthrightly. At the airport, she said, she had hung back because Bourdin "looked odd." She added, "If I went with my gut, I would have known right away." She admitted that she had taken drugs—"probably" heroin, methadone, and alcohol—before the polygraph exam. "When they accused me, I freaked out," she said. "I worked my ass off to raise my kids. Why would I do something to my kids?" She continued, "I'm not a violent person. They didn't talk to any of my friends or associates. . . . It was just a shot in the dark, to see if I'd admit something." She also said of herself, "I'm the world's worst liar. I can't lie worth crap."

I asked her if Jason had hurt Nicholas. She paused for a moment, then said that she didn't think so. She acknowledged that when Jason did cocaine he became "totally wacko—a completely different person—and it was scary." He even beat up his father once, she said. But she noted that Jason had not been a serious addict until after Nicholas disappeared. She agreed with the authorities on one point: she placed little credence in Jason's reported sighting of Nicholas after he disappeared.

"Jason was having problems at that time," she said. "I just don't believe Nicholas came there."

As we spoke, I asked several times how she could have believed for nearly five months that a twenty-three-year-old Frenchman with dyed hair, brown eyes, and a European accent was her son. "We just kept making excuses—that he's different because of all this ugly stuff that had happened," she said. She and Carey wanted it to be him so badly. It was only after he came to live with her that she had doubts. "He just didn't act like my son," Beverly said. "I couldn't bond with him. I just didn't have that feeling. My heart went out for him, but not like a mother's would. The kid's a mess and it's sad, and I wouldn't wish that on anybody."

Beverly's experience, as incredible as it is, does have a precursor—an incident that has been described as one of "the strangest cases in the annals of police history." (It is the basis of a Clint Eastwood movie, "Changeling.") On March 10, 1928, a nine-year-old boy named Walter Collins disappeared in Los Angeles. Six months later, after a nationwide manhunt, a boy showed up claiming that he was Walter and insisting that he had been kidnapped. The police were certain that he was Walter, and a family friend testified that "things the boy said and did would convince anybody" that he was the missing child. When Walter's mother, Christine, went to retrieve her son, however, she did not think it was him. Although the authorities and friends persuaded her to take him home, she brought the boy back to a police station after a few days, insisting, "This is not my son." She later testified, "His teeth were different, his voice was different. . . . His ears were smaller." The authorities thought that she must be suffering emotional distress from her son's disappearance, and had her institutionalized in a psychiatric ward. Even then, she refused to budge. As she told a police captain, "One thing a mother ought to know was the identity of her child." Eight days later, she was released. Evidence soon emerged that her son was likely murdered by a serial killer, and the boy claiming to be her son confessed that he was an eleven-year-old runaway from Iowa who, in his words, thought that it was "fun to be somebody you aren't."

Speaking of the Bourdin case, Fisher said that one thing was certain: "Beverly had to know that wasn't her son."

After several months of investigation, Stick determined that there was no evidence to charge anyone with Nicholas's disappearance. There were no witnesses, no DNA. The authorities could not even say whether Nicholas was dead. Stick concluded that Jason's overdose had all but "precluded the possibility" that the authorities could determine what had happened to Nicholas.

On September 9, 1998, Frédéric Bourdin stood in a San Antonio courtroom and pleaded guilty to perjury, and to obtaining and possessing false documents. This time, his claim that he was merely seeking love elicited outrage. Carey, who had a nervous breakdown after Bourdin was arrested, testified before his sentencing, saying, "He has lied, and lied, and lied again. And to this day he continues to lie. He bears no remorse." Stick denounced Bourdin as a "flesh-eating bacteria," and the judge compared what Bourdin had done—giving a family the hope that their lost child was alive and then shattering it—to murder.

The only person who seemed to have any sympathy for Bourdin was Beverly. She said at the time, "I feel sorry for him. You know, we got to know him, and this kid has been through hell. He has a lot of nervous habits." She told me, "He did a lot of things that took a lot of guts, if you think about it."

The judge sentenced Bourdin to six years—more than three times what was recommended under the sentencing guidelines. Bourdin told the courtroom, "I apologize to all the people in my past, for what I have done. I wish, I wish that you believe me, but I know it's impossible." Whether he was in jail or not, he added, "I am a prisoner of myself."

When I last saw Bourdin, in the spring of 2008, his life had undergone perhaps its most dramatic transformation. He had married a Frenchwoman, Isabelle, whom he had met two years earlier. In her late twenties, Isabelle was slim and pretty and soft-spoken. She was studying to be a lawyer. A victim of family abuse, she had seen Bourdin on television, describing his own abuse and his quest for love, and she had been so moved that she eventually tracked him down. "I told him what interests me in his life wasn't the way he bent the truth but why he did that and the things that he looked for," she said.

Bourdin says that when Isabelle first approached him he thought it must be a joke, but they met in Paris and gradually fell in love. He said that he had never been in a relationship before. "I've always been a wall," he said. "A cold wall." On August 8, 2007, after a year of courtship, they got married at the town hall of a village outside Pau.

Bourdin's mother says that Frédéric invited her and his grandfather to the ceremony, but they didn't go. "No one believed him," she says.

When I saw Isabelle, she was nearly eight months pregnant. Hoping to avoid public attention, she and Frédéric had relocated to Le Mans, and they had moved into a small one-bedroom apartment in an old stone building with wood floors and a window that overlooked a prison. "It reminds me of where I've been," Bourdin said. A box containing the pieces of a crib lay on the floor of the sparsely decorated living room. Bourdin's hair was now cropped, and he was dressed without flamboyance, in jeans and a sweatshirt. He told me that he had got a job in telemarketing. Given his skills at persuasion, he was unusually good at it. "Let's just say I'm a natural," he said.

Most of his family believes that all these changes are merely part of another role, one that will end disastrously for his wife and baby. "You can't just invent yourself as a father," his uncle Jean-Luc Drouart said. "You're not a dad for six days or six months. It is not a character—it is a reality." He added, "I fear for that child."

Bourdin's mother, Ghislaine, says that her son is a "liar and will never change."

After so many years of playing an impostor, Bourdin has left his family and many authorities with the conviction that this is who Frédéric Pierre Bourdin really is: he *is* a chameleon. Within months of being released from prison in the United States and deported to France, in October, 2003, Bourdin resumed playing a child. He even stole the identity of a fourteen-year-old missing French boy named Léo Balley, who had vanished almost eight years earlier, on a camping trip. This time, police did a DNA test that quickly revealed that Bourdin was lying. A psychiatrist who evaluated him concluded, "The prognosis seems more than worrying. . . . We are very pessimistic about modifying these personality traits." (Bourdin, while in prison in America, began reading psychology texts, and jotted down in his journal the following passage: "When confronted with his misconduct the psychopath has enough false sincerity and apparent remorse that he renews hope and trust among his accusers. However, after several repetitions, his convincing show is finally recognized for what it is—a show.")

Isabelle is sure that Bourdin "can change." She said, "I've seen him now for two years, and he is not that person."

At one point, Bourdin touched Isabelle's stomach. "My baby can have three arms and three legs," he said. "It doesn't matter. I don't need my child to be perfect. All I want is that this child feels love." He did not care what his family thought. "They are my shelter," he said of his wife and soon-to-be child. "No one can take that from me."

A month later, Bourdin called and told me that his wife had given birth. "It's a girl," he said. He and Isabelle had named her Athena, for the Greek goddess. "I'm really a father," he said.

I asked if he had become a new person. For a moment, he fell silent. Then he said, "No, this is who I am."

—*August, 2008*